CW00541009

اوكسفورد يونيفرستي بريس
GRATIS
Oxford University Press

AS LEVEL
PSYCHOLOGY
WORKBOOK

AS LEVEL
PSYCHOLOGY
WORKBOOK

CLARE CHARLES
North Leamington School, Leamington Spa

Ψ **Psychology Press**
Taylor & Francis Group

HOVE AND NEW YORK

Published in 2008 by Psychology Press Ltd
27 Church Road, Hove, East Sussex, BN3 2FA

http://www.psypress.com
http://www.a-levelpsychology.co.uk

Simultaneously published in the USA and Canada
by Taylor & Francis Inc
270 Madison Avenue, New York, NY 10016

Psychology Press an imprint of the Taylor & Francis Group, an informa business

© 2008 by Psychology Press Ltd

All rights reserved. No part of this book may be reprinted or
reproduced or utilised in any form or by any electronic,
mechanical, or other means, now known or hereafter invented,
including photocopying and recording, or in any information
storage or retrieval system, without permission in writing from
the publishers.

British Library Cataloguing in Publication Data
A catalogue record for this book is available from the British Library

ISBN 978-1-84169-732-1

Cover design by Richard Massing
Typeset in the UK by RefineCatch Ltd, Bungay, Suffolk
Printed and bound in the UK by Ashford Colour Press

Contents

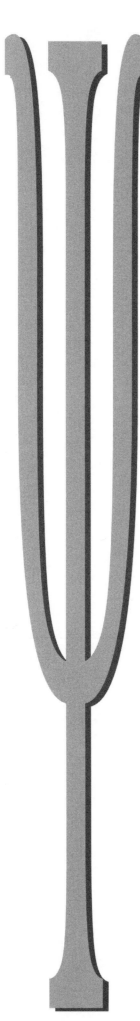

Introduction

Hello

I hope you have begun to think about how to get that C grade or above at AS level psychology. This workbook is here to help you do it. That's no guarantee you'll get the grade you want, of course, because you must use the guide thoroughly to get a good pass. Empty pages mean empty spaces—great big gaps in your knowledge that not even the revision guide will necessarily fill in. This workbook does require some commitment from you—there are notes to be made and model answers to prepare. But then that is the only way to get the AS grade you deserve!

After a brief discussion of the different areas and approaches in the 'What is Psychology?' section that follows, the first section of the workbook is focused on examination skills. The AO1, AO2, and AO3 exam skills are considered in terms of the type of exam question they may be assessed by. There is also a step-by-step guide to answering exam questions in 'Examination Skills'.

Each of the following sections in the workbook corresponds to the six topics on the AS Specification and each section is organised in the same way:

- **Learning objectives** introduce each of the topics. Cross-reference with the Specification so that you can see how the learning objectives meet the requirements of the Specification. Please fill in the self-assessment box on completion of a topic as it is often useful for your own revision and the class programme to have a record of the parts of the Specification that may need close attention during revision.

- **Structured worksheets** that map on to each of the learning objectives. These can be used by you for independent study or be used as a stimulus to guide discussion and note taking in class. The worksheets include page references to Eysenck's *AS Level Psychology, Fourth Edition* textbook and Brody and Dwyer's *Revise AS Level Psychology* revision guide. The worksheets are structured because cues are given that direct note taking and help you to select only the most relevant content. You should be able to cross-reference these cues with the information in most AS textbooks, but they do relate specifically to the Eysenck textbook. Your note taking must be very concise to fit into the worksheets. This is an important skill to acquire because in the exam you will need to be equally succinct.

- **Using this in the exam** will provide guidance on the possible types of exam question for each topic subsection apart from research methods, which has a different revision section appropriate to that topic. There are two subsections per topic on the Specification and so there are two 'Using this in the exam' sections per topic in the workbook, organised immediately after the corresponding notes. These revision sections will cover a range of the short and long answer questions you will experience in the exam, and will include guidance on the possible stimulus questions you may encounter (see more on these types of questions in 'Examination skills'). Essay plans are provided for the extended writing questions that will help you know what to write and how to structure your answers. However, there is no right or wrong answer to the long answer questions and so the plans only provide advice on suitable content and structure; it is up to you how you choose to use them.

Included in the Appendix is a worksheet called 'How to impress the examiner on AO2 and AO3', which provides further ideas on how to do well on the essay questions.

Good luck with your studies. I hope you do get the grade you deserve—make sure you deserve a good one!

Clare Charles

Wherever possible we have provided enough space for you to fill in your answers. However, if you find that there is not enough room to do this, continue on a blank sheet of paper, or use the blank 'Notes' section at the end of the book.

What is Psychology?

Definition of psychology

There are five key areas within psychology: cognitive psychology, developmental psychology, biological psychology, individual differences, and social psychology, and the topics you will study are drawn from these areas. Other areas that exist within the field of psychology include clinical, occupational, comparative, educational, criminal, and neuropsychology. In addition to these main areas, there are various approaches or perspectives to studying psychology: biological, behavioural, cognitive, and psychodynamic, which you will become familiar with during the course of your studies. Each approach takes a different view to explain psychological phenomena. Take a look at the worksheet that follows (see page 5) to find out more about these areas and approaches, which are fundamental to an understanding of psychology.

As you can see, psychology is diverse and challenging and so (nearly) always exciting!!!

Psychologists tend to specialise in a particular area of psychological research, such as children's acquisition of language, the nature and causes of aggression, or the development of moral reasoning. Some psychologists take a particular perspective, but most take an eclectic approach, which means that they draw from a broad range of theories and perspectives rather than being restricted to the approach of only one particular school of thought. This is because *no one theory in science is final*, hence the need to take a multi-perspective approach to studying psychology. This is considered by many to be the only way to deal successfully with the issues that psychologists address. The use of psychology in practical settings is called applied psychology, and the applications are based on research in one or more of the areas; for example, research into problem solving is based on cognitive psychology, and research into prejudice and discrimination is based on social psychology.

Here's a reminder of the five key areas that you are going to study at AS level:

Cognitive   Developmental   Biological   Individual differences   Social

Look at the following applications and see if you can decide which area the application is most likely to be derived from. Discuss this with the people sitting next to you and complete the worksheet with the correct areas. In some cases the application could be based on more than one approach, as a multi-perspective approach may need to be taken, and so you may conclude that it is based on research from more than one of the five areas (detailed on page 5). In these cases write all relevant areas in the boxes below.

Applications

Ψ How to improve memory.

Ψ The causes of schizophrenia.

Ψ What is the basis of interpersonal attraction?

Ψ The relationship between stress and illness.

Ψ Why some people conform and others don't.

Ψ Brain wave activity during sleep.

Ψ The physiological basis of depression.

Ψ Gender differences in socialisation.

Ψ What is normal/is anybody normal?

Ψ Do dreams have meaning or are they just a by-product of brain activity?

Ψ The relationship between the infant and caregiver.

Ψ Artificial intelligence.

Ψ Causes of relationship breakdown.

Ψ Relaxation training.

Ψ Attention deficits.

Ψ Are psychopaths born that way or created by society?

Cognitive psychology

'Cognition' refers to our mental processes, such as attention, perception, thinking, language, and memory. Thus, cognitive psychology looks at how we process information to understand the thoughts that underpin emotions and behaviour. It can overlap with social psychology in the area of social cognition, or with developmental psychology in the area of cognitive development. This approach focuses on the brain as an information processor and computers can be used as an analogy of the brain to help develop mental models to explain and understand cognitive processes.

Developmental psychology

Developmental psychology studies the biological, cognitive, social, and emotional changes that occur throughout the life span. As development is a lifelong process, developmental psychologists start their study with conception and pre-natal development, then move from infancy through to adolescence, adulthood, and finally old age. Topics studied could involve early cognitive development, the attachments formed between infants and their caregivers, and the gender roles acquired in early childhood. The psychodynamic perspective links well to this area because it claims that unconscious childhood conflicts shape adult behaviour.

Biological psychology

Biological psychology aims to establish the biological basis of behaviour. Body structures and functions, in particular brain processing, are investigated to see how they relate to behaviour. For example, the body's response to stress is a good illustration of a behaviour that has a biological basis. Biological psychologists study topics such as how the nerves function, how hormones affect behaviour, and how the different areas of the brain are specialised and related to different behaviours.

Individual differences

As expected, individual differences looks at the wide variation in individuals. It deals with studying the ways in which individuals differ in their psychological characteristics, and this will affect their intelligence, aggressiveness, willingness to conform, masculinity and femininity, and just about every other behaviour you can think of. An important individual difference is the degree to which a person is mentally healthy, and this gives rise to the study of abnormal psychology. However, what is considered to be normal for one person may not be considered to be normal by another person. This means that there is huge controversy and ambiguity in defining abnormality. Within abnormal psychology mental disorders are investigated such as eating disorders, schizophrenia, depression, and anxiety disorders.

Social psychology

'Social' refers to any situation involving two or more members of the same species. Social psychology investigates social interactions, such as interpersonal relationships, group behaviour, leadership, social influence, and the influence of the media. A social psychologist studying interpersonal relationships might study what we find attractive in others or what causes relationships to deteriorate and end. One who is studying social influence might look at how others influence us, e.g., conformity and obedience to authority.

Examination Skills

This study guide provides a framework for useful learning and revision (the worksheets) and advice on how to develop the skills that will be assessed in the examination (the AO1 and AO2 revision summaries). AO1, AO2, and AO3 are the skills being assessed and what follows reveals exactly what these requirements are and how to achieve highly on all three assessment objectives.

The exam format

Unit 1	Unit 2
1½ hours	1½ hours
AO1 16.66%	AO1 20.83%
AO2 16.66%	AO2 20.83%
AO3 16.66%	AO3 8.33%

Questions consist of short answer questions, stimulus material questions, and long answer questions.

Short answer and stimulus material questions are variable in how many marks each question carries, but tend to range from 1–6 marks. You can receive marks for AO1, AO2, and AO3 in these questions.

The long answer questions include at least one 12-mark question, which is split 50 : 50 between AO1 and AO2. You do not gain AO3 marks for the long answer questions. Unit 1 will always contain only one 12-mark question and Unit 2 may contain one or more. There are also 8-mark answers, again split 50 : 50 between AO1 and AO2. Usually, your long answer questions will consist of two paragraphs: one for AO1 marks and one for AO2 marks. (Conclusions are not required for the long answer questions as these would weight the marks too much in favour of AO2.)

Ψ AO1 tests knowledge and understanding of science and of *How Science Works*

You may be asked to:

- Ψ Recognise, recall, and show understanding of content.
- Ψ Select, organise, and communicate content in a variety of forms.

Ψ AO2 Application of knowledge and understanding of science and of *How Science Works*

You may be asked to:

- Ψ Analyse and evaluate scientific knowledge and processes.
- Ψ Apply scientific knowledge and processes to content and issues raised.
- Ψ Assess the validity, reliability, and credibility of scientific information.

Ψ AO3 How Science Works

You may be asked to:

- Ψ Describe ethical, safe, and skilful practical techniques and processes, selecting appropriate qualitative and quantitative data.
- Ψ Know how to make, record, and communicate reliable and valid observations and measurements with appropriate precision and accuracy, through using primary and secondary sources.
- Ψ Analyse, interpret, explain, and evaluate the methodology, results, and impact of experimental research.

This will be examined across both AS units but there are more questions in Unit 1 due to Research Methods being part of this exam paper, as the above breakdown of the skills across the two units shows.

Quality of written communication (QWC)

There are two marks per unit paper, for good use of grammar and punctuation, correct spelling, legible handwriting, appropriate style of writing, clear expression, and accurate use of technical terms. This should pose few problems for an AS level student! It will be assessed in the extended 12-mark questions.

Types of exam questions

Stimulus questions: In these questions you will be required to recognise content and show your understanding of it. This could be in terms of AO1 (identify content), AO2 (explain the content), or AO3 (consider methodological and ethical issues that relate to the content in the stimulus).

Example question

1. Using the list below, complete the table to distinguish between long-term memory and short-term memory.

- Unlimited
- Up to a lifetime
- 7 +/− 2 items
- Mainly acoustic
- Seconds
- Mainly semantic

	Short-term memory (STM)	Long-term memory (LTM)
Capacity		
Duration		
Encoding		

Short answer questions: These questions range from 1–6 marks and will require you either to outline content (AO1), explain content and differences between content (AO2), or consider the methodological and ethical issues that relate to the content (AO3).

Example questions

AO1 questions

1. Outline research into obedience. (5 marks)
2. Outline key features of the multi-store model. (6 marks)

AO2 questions

1. Explain factors that increase resistance to obedience. (6 marks)
2. Select two definitions of abnormality and explain one limitation of each definition. (2 + 2 marks)

AO3 questions

1. Explain why studies of eyewitness testimony have been criticised as lacking validity. (5 marks)
2. (a) Explain one disadvantage of using an interview to collect data. (2 marks)
   (b) Write one question that could be used as part of the interview that would generate qualitative data. (2 marks)

Long answer questions: These will be 8 or 12 marks. The 12-mark question in particular you should answer as a mini-essay and structure as two paragraphs because you will be assessed for the quality of your written language. The questions consist of 50 : 50 AO1 to AO2 skills so make sure that you include both description/outline of content as AO1; and explanation, commentary, analysis, and evaluation of content as AO2.

Example questions

1. Consider whether criticisms of the validity of obedience research are justified. (8 or 12 marks)
2. Discuss the use of drugs to manage the negative effects of stress. (8 or 12 marks)
3. Outline and evaluate one explanation of attachment. (8 or 12 marks)
4. Outline the multi-store model of memory and give strengths and weaknesses of this model. (8 or 12 marks)

Mark schemes

Note that these generic mark schemes would be adapted depending on whether the question was 3, 4, 5, or 6 marks.

Mark scheme for short answer AO1 questions

6 marks	Accurate and reasonably detailed
4–5 marks	Less detailed but generally accurate
3–2 marks	Basic
1 mark	Very brief/flawed or inappropriate
0 marks	No creditworthy material

Mark scheme for short answer AO2 questions

6 marks	Effective explanation/evaluation
4–5 marks	Reasonable explanation/evaluation
3–2 marks	Basic explanation/evaluation
1 mark	Rudimentary explanation/evaluation
0 marks	No creditworthy material

Mark scheme for short answer AO3 questions

There is no generic mark scheme for AO3 questions as the application of the mark scheme is variable depending on the way in which your understanding of how science works is being assessed.

Mark scheme for 12-mark questions

Simply combine the 6-mark schemes for AO1 and AO2 together for the long answer questions.

Step-by-step Guide to Answering Exam Questions

Cross-reference this with the Specification, the 'Using this in the exam' sections on the worksheets, and see the 'Examination Skills' pages for further information on the types of exam question.

There are two exam papers:

PSY1: Memory, Attachments, and Research Methods
PSY2: Stress, Social Influence, and Abnormality

The exam structure is variable but you must answer ALL the questions and answer them in the lined space provided (the exam board will not mark answers given outside the lined space). The total marks = 72 and you have 90 minutes to answer, which means you have just over a minute per mark. The questions consist of three types: the stimulus questions, the short answer, and the long answer, as detailed in 'Examination Skills'.

As with all exams there are ways to ensure you achieve the very best grade:

1. **Read the questions carefully.** So nothing difficult there! But do this strategically. Think about how many marks the question carries and match the amount you write to this. Look at the exam injunction (outline, describe, evaluate) and if asked to outline/describe do not include criticisms and if asked to give criticisms do not describe.

2. **Use the mark allocation.** The length of your answer must be in proportion to the marks available, so make sure that this is the first thing that you check so that you give an appropriate amount of detail. Don't write too little (one sentence for a 3-mark answer is likely to fall below 'pass standard') and don't write too much. Particularly watch out for writing too much as this will penalise your ability to answer later questions as there is simply not enough time for extra material, i.e., do not spend 10 minutes on a 6-mark question as you will lose out elsewhere.

3. **Watch the time.** You only have just over 1 minute per mark.

4. **Label you answers.** The examiner should have no difficulty working out which question you have answered so it must be numbered clearly, e.g., Q1 (a), (b), (c). Also, if two explanations, factors, or criticisms are asked for number these i) and ii). Don't leave it to the examiner to work out which is point one and which is point two —you want them to be in a good mood.

5. **Read through your answers.** Do this if you are sitting waiting for the exam to end, which is unlikely to happen given the tight time limits. But if you do have some spare time, check for spelling and grammar as you can lose marks on this. Also check the accuracy of your answers and if there is anything else you could possibly add in.

6. **Essay technique.** The 12-mark and 8-mark questions are mini-essay questions and so you should attempt to structure your answer as an essay.

   i) **Structure**—The two-paragraph model is a useful way to achieve structure and get the correct ratio of 50 AO1:50 AO2, as the first paragraph can be AO1 and the next AO2. Aim to write in total 200+ words with approximately 100 words per paragraph on the 12-mark questions; and 150+ words with approximately 75 words per paragraph on the 8-mark questions.

   Paragraph 1: AO1 100–120 words, approximate time 8 minutes and must aim for 6 marks.

   Show you understand the question by identifying the main features of whatever the question has asked you to consider. Don't begin with a description of lots of studies as this often results in a mainly AO1 answer, so save the research for AO2.

   Paragraph 2: AO2 100–120 words, approximate time 8 minutes and must aim for 6 marks.

   Research evidence in support, i.e., the arguments for and/or positive criticisms; the 'pros'. Avoid description by limiting content on research evidence to findings/conclusions. Use link sentences, e.g., 'The findings/conclusions support… because they show that…' and move onto research evidence that contradicts/challenges, i.e., the arguments against and/or negative criticisms; the 'cons'.

Make sure that any research you cite in paragraph 2 is phrased as AO2, e.g. 'This research suggests…because the findings show…' and then give your own conclusions to keep your answer evaluative. Remember if you question the validity you are questioning the truth, which reduces the value of the research. Thus, validity is crucial in weighing up the evidence for and against and assessing research contributions/insights.

This is a useful framework but you don't have to be as prescriptive as this; note how some of the model essays take this structure but others vary slightly. Try to see the essay question as something a friend has just asked your advice about. So to begin with you need to offer some knowledge and understanding (AO1) but not too much to bore them senseless! Next you're going to consider both sides of the argument, i.e., debate the pros and cons and then give your conclusion.

ii) **Selective use of material** —Don't write everything you know about a subject, certainly don't describe too much, as you need only enough for half of the marks. Be selective—the material you include should be only the most relevant material. This is something you need to have practised before the exam, i.e., prepare model answers.

iii) **Evaluation and analysis** —Discussing strengths and weaknesses, the scientific process, applications of the research, and the validity, reliability, and credibility of psychological concepts all constitute evaluation. Analysis requires you to break down the question, which can be done by looking at the arguments for and against whatever the question is suggesting.

iv) **Psychologically informed** —Whilst you may well have your own opinion in answer to the question, it is vital that you back this up with psychological research and theory. This is true of any exam question, be it short answer or essay; you need psychological research/theory so that your answer is more than the 'man on the street' answer! You can use this to support or contradict the argument you are making. Use the research you write about on the worksheets to inform your answer. It is *essential* that you include *link sentences* here, e.g., this research supports, contradicts, illustrates, etc. to make your content evaluative, not descriptive.

v) **Does your answer have MERIT?**

   Methodological criticisms—Criticise the research method and assess what that means in terms of the validity of the research. Usually this means the research lacks validity (internal and/or external), which reduces the meaningfulness of the findings.

   Ethical—Do the ends justify the means? Are the findings socially sensitive?

   Real-life validity, i.e., explanatory power, applications, contextualise —Does the research/theory work in real life and so have value, truth, and validity? Research that lacks internal validity is unlikely to generalise to real life, which means it lacks ecological validity (a form of external validity). Consider the benefits (applications) of the research. Consider the extent to which the research is dated because it is a product of the time and context (historical, political, social, and cultural) when it was conducted and so lacks external validity (temporal, ecological, and population validity) to the current context.

   Individual, social, and cultural diversity—Consider if these are accounted for. Or do participant variables/individual differences limit the generalisability of research?

   Theoretical criticisms—Consider reductionism and determinism, nature/nurture.

vi) **Remember it takes practice, practice, practice… and more practice!**

Memory Learning Objectives

On completion of this topic you should be familiar with the following.

Models of memory

- Describe short-term memory (STM) and long-term memory (LTM).
- Distinguish between STM and LTM in terms of encoding, capacity, and duration and be able to define these terms.
- Describe and evaluate the multi-store model and the working memory model, including strengths and weaknesses.

Memory in everyday life

- Outline and evaluate research into eyewitness testimony (EWT).
- Critically consider the factors affecting the accuracy of EWT, including anxiety and age of witness.
- Discuss the effect of misleading information on EWT.
- Explain the use of the cognitive interview and assess its effectiveness.
- Discuss strategies for improving memory.

Cross-reference the above learning objectives with the Specification and fill in the self-assessment box below on completion of the topic.

SELF-ASSESSMENT BOX
☺   **Which of the above do you know?**
☹   **Are there any gaps in your knowledge that need to be targeted during revision?**

STM and LTM

For details, see Eysenck's textbook (pages 43–53) and Brody and Dwyer's revision guide (page 16). Use the cues in the tables to guide your note taking and fill in the gaps using the letter clues provided.

Two types of memory have been identified; s_____-term memory (STM) and l_____-term memory (LTM) and these are generally considered to be memory structures or stores of information.

STM: This is our present conscious experience where information is processed through attention and rehearsal. Hence, it is also called working memory. Information is s_____ temporarily and it is thought to have limited c_____ and d_____.

LTM: Information can be stored p_____, for example, people can remember childhood memories in old age. It is thought to have u_____ capacity and duration if information has been processed sufficiently. The complexity and variety of LTM has led to different types of memory being identified, e.g., d_____ (memory for facts) and p_____ (memory for skills).

To use a computer analogy, STM is the RAM and LTM is the ROM.

The structure of memory definitions	
Short-term memory	**Long-term memory**

Encoding: The transfer of information into c_____, which creates a m_____ trace that can be registered in the memory store. STM and LTM are dependent on different codes, as in STM encoding it is primarily a_____ (based on the sound of the word) and in LTM it is primarily s_____ (based on the meaning of the word).

Capacity: A m_____ of how much is held in memory. The term span measure is used as an assessment of how much can be s_____d in short-term memory at any time. It is generally agreed that the span of short-term memory is 'seven, plus or minus two' chunks of information, where the units can be numbers, letters, or words, whereas the capacity of LTM is potentially un_____d.

Duration: This refers to how long a memory l_____s. The existence of two distinct memory stores is supported by duration because this differs between STM and LTM. STM has a very limited duration of 18–30 s_____s, whereas LTM potentially lasts forever and so a memory may endure p_____y.

EXAM TIP: You may be asked in the exam to distinguish between STM and LTM. The easiest way to do this is to compare encoding, capacity, and duration. The research on encoding, capacity, and duration supports the concept that STM and LTM are separate stores, and therefore the structure proposed by the multi-store model, which is the next area of study.

Store	Encoding	Capacity	Duration
STM			
LTM			
Differences between STM and LTM			

Find out for yourself: Try testing the capacity and duration of STM for yourself. Read about Jacobs' (1887) span measure test and the Brown–Peterson technique in the textbook and design your own research to replicate these studies.

Models of Memory

For details, see Eysenck's textbook (pages 43–61) and Brody and Dwyer's revision guide (pages 15–22). Use the cues in the tables to guide your note taking.

Multi-store model—Atkinson and Shiffrin (1968)

Description

Fill in the gaps using your textbook and the letter clues provided.

According to the multi-store model there are three memory stores. Information enters s_____ m_____. There is one sensory store for each s_____ modality, therefore one for v_____, one for h_____, etc. The sensory store is overwhelmed with information and so it is only information that is attended to that enters s_____-t_____ m_____. Information cannot be held long in STM as it has limited c_____ and d_____. Information is transferred from STM to LTM through r_____ (verbal r_____). Without r_____ it is l_____. The more something is r_____, the stronger the m_____ trace. This model emphasises s_____ (the three stores) and p_____ (attention and rehearsal).

Positive evaluation

Research evidence to support the theory:

Ψ Differences in encoding, capacity, and duration between STM and LTM.

Ψ Recency effects. See Glanzer and Cunitz's (1966) research.

Ψ Case studies of brain damaged patients, e.g., HM, and see Shallice and Warrington's (1970) findings.

Negative evaluation

Ψ Rehearsal is not essential for the transfer of information into LTM and the emphasis placed on this may be a consequence of the artificiality of memory experiments. See Hyde and Jenkins' (1973) study of incidental learning. Consider flashbulb memory.

Ψ STM and LTM are not single stores and it is questionable whether they are separate stores.

Ψ It is an active not a passive process (see the working memory model, which does consider STM to be an active processor); a two-way not one-way transfer of information.

Ψ Are STM and LTM separate stores?

Ψ Artificiality of research may exaggerate the STM/LTM distinction and the importance of rehearsal.

Find out for yourself: Replicate the recency effect research. Does your data form the serial position curve? Explain how this research supports the multi-store model.

Working memory model—Baddeley and Hitch (1974)

Description

Fill in the gaps using your textbook and the letter clues provided.

This expands on the multi-store model's over-simplistic representation of STM as a s_____ store. According to the working memory model, STM is an active store made up of three components. It consists of the a_____ -p_____ l_____ for acoustic memories, the v_____-s_____ s_____ p_____ for visual memories, and the c_____ e_____ controls the different slave systems and attention.

GRATIS

Oxford University Press

Positive evaluation

Research evidence to support the theory:

Ψ Hitch and Baddeley (1976).

Ψ Evidence for the phonological loop.

Ψ Evidence for the visuo-spatial sketchpad.

Ψ Evidence for the central executive.

Ψ The working memory model provides a more advanced account of memory than the multi-store model because it explains better real-life memory abilities.

Negative evaluation

Ψ We still lack an understanding of key concepts, e.g., the central executive.

Ψ The working memory model is also an oversimplified account of memory as there is still much to be explained about the functioning of working memory.

Find out for yourself: Try investigating some of the processes involved in comprehension by using the detailed guidance provided in Eysenck's textbook on page 55.

Using this in the exam: Models of memory

You may be asked:

Short answer AO1 questions

1. Recognise differences between STM and LTM as presented in a stimulus question.
2. Describe key concepts of the multi-store model or working memory model, for example, the structure or the processes.
3. Outline the concepts of encoding, capacity, and duration.

Short answer AO2 questions

1. Give strengths and weaknesses of the multi-store model or working memory model.

Short answer AO3 questions

1. Explain why research lacks validity, for example, the research into the differences between STM and LTM.
2. Explain how the working memory model differs from the multi-store model.

Long answer questions

These can be either 8 marks or 12 marks, where AO1: AO2 is 50 : 50, so be prepared to give a shorter or longer version of this answer depending on whether the question is 8 or 12 marks. Use the plans as a guide but be prepared to adapt your answer if you're asked for just strengths or weaknesses, as opposed to both.

1. Outline the multi-store model of memory and give strengths and weaknesses of this model. (8 or 12 marks)

Paragraph 1 Describe the key features of the model.

Outline the main features including the three stores, differences between STM and LTM, and process of rehearsal.

Paragraph 2 Provide evidence for and against the model.

Research that demonstrates differences in encoding, capacity, and duration between STM and LTM supports this distinction as identified by the multi-store model. Further research evidence in support of the multi-store model includes Murdock's serial position curve and Glanzer and Cunitz's research using an interference task that supported the importance of rehearsal.

The multi-store model is oversimplified because STM and LTM are not single stores. The working memory model shows that there are different types of memory in STM and research has also shown that LTM is not a single store, as declarative and procedural have been identified. Also, there is the case of 'HM', which demonstrated that rehearsal may also be an oversimplification as he was able to form new STM and hold it there, i.e., rehearsal, but was not able to transfer this information to LTM. Hence, this case study suggests the mechanism may be more complex than simply rehearsal. Certainly rehearsal is not always necessary for memories to become permanent, e.g., flashbulb memory. The multi-store model is also criticised because it portrays STM and LTM as passive stores when they are active processors. The working memory model demonstrated this is true of STM and so it expanded on the multi-store model to improve on its reductionism.

2. Outline the working memory model and give strengths and weaknesses of this model. (8 or 12 marks)

Paragraph 1 Describe the key features of the model.

Outline the main features of this model including the central executive, which controls the slave systems, the articulatory-phonological loop, and the visuo-spatial sketchpad.

Paragraph 2 Provide evidence for and against the model.

Research that supports the model is based on research using the dual-task technique, e.g., Hitch and Baddeley (1976) and Baddeley and Lewis (1981). Positive criticisms include the fact that it recognises STM as an active processor and that it is not a single passive unit. The practical applications of the model are a strength, for example, it explains verbal reasoning, mental arithmetic, reading, and planning and so can be applied to improve these abilities. Negative criticisms include the fact that not a great deal is known about the central executive; it is difficult to verify an abstract concept. It is probably an oversimplification to see the central executive as one system. Only the articulatory-phonological loop has been explored in any detail and so research is lacking on the visuo-spatial sketchpad.

Eyewitness Testimony

For details, see Eysenck's textbook (pages 63–69) and Brody and Dwyer's revision guide (pages 23–25). Fill in the gaps using the letter clues and use the cues in the table to guide your note taking.

Eyewitness testimony (EWT) is a major application of our knowledge of m_____. EWT is likely to rely on r_____ memory and the worksheet on this explains why reconstruction decreases the reliability of EWT. The evidence for the u_____ of EWT is considerable . For example, the Devlin report (1976) advised that convictions should not be based on EWT alone. However, EWT remains an issue because juries are highly influenced by it. Reconstruction is not the only source of distortion in EWT; the language used, in particular l_____ q_____, can b_____ eyewitness testimony.

Definition of eyewitness testimony (EWT)

Age of the witness	
Ψ Children vs. adults (Pozzulo & Lindsay, 1998).	Ψ Older eyewitnesses are more influenced by misleading suggestions. Use Mueller-Johnson and Ceci (2004) and Dodson and Krueger (2006) as evidence.
Ψ Younger children are more suggestible (Bronfenbrenner, 1988).	
	Ψ Own age bias (Wright & Stroud, 2002).
Ψ Cognitive incompetence (Bruck & Melnyk, 2004).	
Ψ How do Gross and Hayne (1999) suggest the accuracy of EWT by young eyewitnesses can be improved?	Ψ How can the accuracy of EWT by older eyewitnesses be improved?

Anxiety of the witness	
Ψ Weapon focus effect (Loftus, 1979).	**Evaluation** Ψ Weapon focus may lack validity.
Ψ The effects of anxiety and stress on face identification (Deffenbacher et al., 2004).	Ψ Why might laboratory findings exaggerate the inaccuracy of EWT?
Ψ Individual differences in anxiety (Bothwell et al., 1987).	Ψ How do Ihlebaek et al. (2003) challenge the above through their findings that laboratory conditions may underestimate errors?

Misleading Information

For details, see Eysenck's textbook (pages 69–71) and Brody and Dwyer's revision guide (pages 25–28). Use the cues in the table to guide your note taking.

The effect of language on recall	
Ψ Leading questions (Loftus & Palmer, 1974).	**Evaluation** Ψ Minor details vs. central details (Heath & Erickson, 1998).
Ψ Post-event information – 'a' vs. 'the' (Loftus & Zanni, 1975).	Ψ Artificiality means external validity is low and so research may not generalise to real-life EWT. Yuille and Cutshall (1986) found much higher accuracy and reliability in real-life EWT.
Ψ EWT can be distorted by misleading information presented *before* the event (Lindsay et al., 2004).	

Find out for yourself: Replicate Loftus's research. You could test 'smashed vs. hit' and the definite article 'a' vs. the indefinite article 'the'. Use the descriptions of these studies in Eysenck's textbook to find out how to design these studies.

Reconstructive Memory

For details, see Eysenck's textbook (pages 71–72) and Brody and Dwyer's revision guide (pages 28–30). Fill in the gaps using the letter clues provided and use the cues in the table to guide your note taking.

Reconstruction is the a_____ process used to r_____ memories as people do not have total recall. R_____ consist of real elements of a memory and g_____ in memory that people fill in based on their knowledge of the world (called s_____). Thus, schemas lead to d_____ and this explains why eyewitness testimony (EWT) is u_____. To use a jigsaw as an analogy, some bits are 'real' pieces and some bits are 'made-up', which does not provide an accurate picture of the witnessed event.

Definition of reconstructive memory

Bartlett's (1932) repeated reproduction method— 'The War of the Ghosts'

Ψ Why was the story from an unfamiliar culture?

Ψ What distortions were evident in the reconstructions?

Evaluation

Ψ The research lacked objectivity, which means it may be subject to researcher bias and other factors may have affected memory.

Ψ High ecological validity as the task is generalisable to everyday memory demands.

Ψ Schema theory fails to make clear predictions.

The Cognitive Interview

For details, see Eysenck's textbook (pages 72–74) and Brody and Dwyer's revision guide (page 30). Use the cues in the table to guide your note taking and fill in the gaps using the letter clues.

Positive applications of the research that have improved the accuracy of EWT
Implications for police procedures Ψ Improvements in interview techniques were suggested in Home Office guidelines.
The basic cognitive interview (Geiselman et al., 1985) Ψ How effective is the basic cognitive interview in comparison to the standard police interview?
The enhanced cognitive interview (Fisher et al., 1987) Ψ How does the effectiveness of the enhanced cognitive interview compare with that of the basic interview?

Assess the reliability and accuracy of EWT and effectiveness of the cognitive interview
Research suggests that the language used can d_____ the information that is stored and retrieved, that is l_____ q_____ can bias EWT. Leading questions can have a suggestibility effect as they can falsely suggest information. This supports Bartlett's (1932) r_____ approach to memory as the research on EWT suggests that EWT involves active reconstruction, where prior knowledge (s_____) can lead to memory distortions at storage and retrieval. Also post-event i_____ and memory b_____ may further distort information. However, the research evidence is based on l_____ e_____ and it may well be the case that real-life EWT is much more a_____ than this would suggest. The c_____ i_____ (CI) does increase the a_____ of information elicited in EWT, but there are concerns about the a_____ of the information; the CI is less effective over longer t_____ intervals; and it is not entirely clear whether all of the many components of the CI contribute to its s_____.

Other factors that influence the accuracy of EWT	
Witness factors—characteristics Ψ Arousal of the witness.	**Event factors—to do with the situation** Ψ Exposure time.
Ψ Cultural stereotypes of the witness.	Ψ Weapon focus.
Ψ Familiarity/knowledge of suspect helps with face recognition.	Ψ Time between event and recording of the EWT.

Memory Improvement

For details, see Eysenck's textbook (pages 74–86) and Brody and Dwyer's revision guide (pages 31–36). Fill in the gaps using the letter clues and use the cues in the table to guide your note taking.

Pre-existing knowledge makes it much easier to o_____ the information you are trying to learn. However, organisation is not the only factor, relating new learning to prior k_____ is also an effective way to improve m_____. The importance of organisation is shown by research where memory is i_____ when the information is o_____. Moreover, even when the information is not organised research shows we have a powerful tendency to i_____ organisation onto new information. M_____ techniques are often cited as dramatically increasing memory; these are mainly based on v_____ i_____ or they are word- b_____. These techniques combine o_____ and p_____ k_____ as part of the technique to improve memory.

Organisation	
Organisation in the learning material (Schuell, 1969) Ψ What were the two conditions of this study? Ψ There are three key findings: 1) 2) 3) Ψ Organisation during learning (Weist, 1972).	**The effect of hierarchy (Bower et al., 1969)** Ψ How many times greater was recall in the organised than in the random condition? Ψ How does Bower's research illustrate the importance of hierarchy?

Organising random words

Mandler's (1967) research
Ψ What were the procedures of this study?

Ψ What were the findings of this study?

Evaluation of Mandler's research
Ψ Did a lack of random allocation bias the results?

Ψ Participants were excluded from analysis.

Ψ Time may be a confounding variable.

Organisation may be offset by the effect of reconstructive memory (Bartlett, 1932) and the consequent false memory effect. Use research evidence to support this.

Find out for yourself: You can test the effect of organisation by carrying out the research suggested on page 75 of Eysenck's textbook.

Mnemonic techniques

Method of loci—a visual imagery technique
Ψ How does this technique work?

Evaluation
Ψ Evidence for the effectiveness of the method.

Ψ External validity has been questioned and defended (De Beni et al., 1997).

Ψ Less effective with abstract information.

Ψ If the information to be learned is presented visually this interferes with the technique.

Ψ Less effective with more complex, integrated information.

Ψ Why is recall usually not immediate?

The pegword method—a visual imagery technique

Ψ How does this technique work?

Evaluation

Ψ Evidence for the effectiveness of the method.

Ψ Requires extensive training.

Ψ Better with concrete than abstract information.

Ψ External validity.

Ψ Interference can reduce the effect of the technique.

Verbal mnemonics

Ψ Acronym.

Ψ Acrostic.

Story method—a word-based technique

Ψ How does this technique work?

Evaluation

Ψ Evidence for the effectiveness of the method.

Ψ Requires extensive training.

Ψ Difficult to use when information is presented rapidly.

Ψ Little real-world usefulness.

Why do mnemonic techniques work?

According to Ericsson (1988), there are three requirements to high memory ability and these illustrate why the mnemonics work:

1) Meaningful encoding

2) Retrieval structure

3) Speed-up

Mind maps

Ψ What is a mind-map?

Ψ Evidence for the effectiveness of mind-maps.

General evaluation of improving memory techniques

Ψ The techniques are effective.

Ψ Organisation and pre-existing knowledge combine effectively in most of the techniques.

Ψ The notion of 'organisation' is vague.

Ψ Lack of understanding of the nature of pre-existing knowledge used.

Ψ Limited application—although not true of all the method of loci, has been used with more complex information.

Evaluation

Ψ Individual differences (Budd, 2004).

Ψ Advantages of mind maps over note-taking.

Ψ Why are they effective?

Find out for yourself: Test the effectiveness of the pegword method by following the procedures detailed on page 81 of Eysenck's textbook.

Using this in the exam: Memory in everyday life

You may be asked:

Short answer AO1 questions

1. Identify/outline factors that affect EWT.
2. Outline research into misleading information.
3. Outline the key features of the cognitive interview.
4. Outline strategies for memory improvement.

Short answer AO2 questions

1. Explain how a person could improve their recall.
2. Evaluate research into misleading information.

Short answer AO3 questions

1. Explain why research lacks validity, for example research into EWT.
2. Explain how the cognitive interview improves the reliability and validity of EWT.

Long answer questions

These can be either 8 marks or 12 marks, where AO1 : AO2 is 50 : 50 so be prepared to give a shorter or longer version of this answer depending on whether the question is 8 or 12 marks.

1. Critically consider to what extent research has improved the reliability of eyewitness testimony. (8 or 12 marks)

Paragraph 1 AO1 Show you understand the question.
Identify research that has suggested ways to improve the reliability of EWT. For example, the effect of reconstruction (Bartlett, 1932), leading questions, and post-event information, which can lead to memory blending (Loftus's research) and so it is research into these areas that has yielded insights into ways to improve the reliability of EWT.

Paragraph 2 AO2 Evidence for and against.
Provide evidence that research has improved police procedures and then evidence against by questioning the validity and so usefulness of the research.

Research on EWT has had a positive impact on police procedures. For example, the cognitive interview has been developed based on Loftus's findings on leading questions and post-event information, which suggests interviews should progress from free recall, to open questions, to closed questions to reduce the potential for bias. Research suggests the cognitive interview yields twice as many correct statements as the standard police interview (Geiselman et al., 1985) and so this has improved the reliability and validity of EWT.

However, the validity of the above insights into sources of bias can be questioned. Although Loftus and Palmer (1974) and Loftus and Zanni (1975) have demonstrated the effect of leading questions and post-event information, as their research was carried out in the artificial conditions of the lab, it may lack external validity and so caution must be taken in generalising these findings to real-life EWT. The extent to which EWT testimony needs to be improved can also be questioned as real-life EWT has higher accuracy than the research would suggest. Yuille and Cutshall (1986) have found impressive accuracy in people's recall of the main events of a crime. Furthermore, research suggests that it is easier to distort minor details than key details, which raises further doubt as to what extent improvements need to be made in real-life EWT. Thus, the extent to which psychological research can improve the reliability of EWT is limited because of the methodological weaknesses of the research.

Early Social Development
Learning Objectives

On completion of this topic you should be familiar with the following.

Attachment

- Critically consider the individual variation in types of attachment identified by Ainsworth's Strange Situation research and the three types of attachment found in this, including the distinction between secure and insecure attachment.
- Describe and evaluate cross-cultural variations in attachment.
- Discuss the explanations of attachment: learning theory, the evolutionary perspective and Bowlby's attachment theory.
- Critically consider disruption of attachment, failure to form attachment (privation), and the effects of institutionalisation.

Attachment in everyday life

- Discuss the impact of different forms of day care on children's social development including the effects on aggression and peer relations.
- Assess the implications of research into attachment and day care for child care practices.

Cross-reference the above learning objectives with the Specification and fill in the self-assessment box below on completion of the topic.

SELF-ASSESSMENT BOX

☺ **Which of the above do you know?**

☹ **Are there any gaps in your knowledge that need to be targeted during revision?**

Attachments in Development

For details, see Eysenck's textbook (pages 91–94) and Brody and Dwyer's revision guide (pages 39–42). Fill in the gaps using the letter clues provided and use the cues in the table to guide your note taking.

Ask yourself: 'What makes my life meaningful?' The two most common answers are f_____ and r_____ partners. Bowlby (1969) suggests that early a_____ are a basis for all future relationships, as an i_____ w_____ m_____ about relationships is formed. Whilst this should not be accepted without question, it does demonstrate the significance of our e_____ attachments.

Maccoby's (1980) key characteristics of attachment
Ψ Seeking proximity to primary caregiver.
Ψ Distress on separation (separation anxiety).
Ψ Pleasure when reunited.
Ψ General orientation of behaviour towards primary caregiver.

Why do infants form attachments?	
Short-term benefits	**Long-term benefits**

Find out for yourself: Think of the key characteristics of your attachments to family and friends. How do these compare with the characteristics suggested by Maccoby (1980)?

Types of Attachment

For details, see Eysenck's textbook (pages 94–102) and Brody and Dwyer's revision guide (pages 43–53). Fill in the gaps using the letter clues provided and use the cues in the table to guide your note taking.

The S_____ S_____ is a controlled observation study designed by A_____ and B_____ (1970) as a measure of a_____. By placing infants in conditions of high and low stress in an unfamiliar environment—the Strange Situation—they tested the q_____ of the infant's attachment to its c_____ whilst the infant was aged between _____ and _____ months.

The Strange Situation (Ainsworth & Bell, 1970)

Ψ What key behaviours are measured in the Strange Situation as indicators of attachment?

- ....

- ....

- ....

Definition of secure attachment

Definition of insecure attachment

Secure attachment type

Secure (70%) Type B

Insecure attachment types

Avoidant (20%) Type A

Resistant (10%) Type C

Disorganised Type D

Ψ This attachment type was suggested by Main and Soloman (1986) as a criticism of the attachment types identified by Ainsworth and Bell.

Evaluation of the Strange Situation

Reliability = consistency

Ψ How is reliability tested?

Ψ Research evidence (Wartner et al., 1994).

Validity = truth

Ψ Criterion validity.

Ψ Research evidence (Stams, Juffer, & van IJzendoorn, 2002).

Ψ The research demonstrates a correlation not causation between attachment and later social development. Why?

Strengths	Weaknesses
Ψ Why is the Strange Situation (SS) a good measure of attachment?	Ψ Why is the disorganised Type D a criticism of Ainsworth's SS research?
Ψ What are the positive implications of secure attachment?	Ψ Ethnocentric and an imposed etic.
Ψ What conclusion can be made about the reliability and validity of the SS as a measure of attachment?	Ψ How might the artificiality of the research affect validity of the attachment types?
Ψ How has the SS extended our knowledge?	Ψ A reductionist classification.

Alternative explanations for individual differences

The temperament hypothesis (Kagan, 1984)	The maternal sensitivity hypothesis (Ainsworth, 1982)	Transactional model An interaction of the infant's innate temperament and the sensitivity of the caregiver.

Cross-cultural Variations in Attachment Types

For details, see Eysenck's textbook (pages 112–115) and Brody and Dwyer's revision guide (pages 53–54). Fill in the gaps using the letter clues provided and use the cues in the table to guide your note taking.

The S_____ S_____ has been used to investigate attachment t_____ in countries other than A_____, where Ainsworth developed the method. If attachment is in_____ then the attachment types should be fairly u_____.

Definition of cross-cultural variations

Cross-cultural variations in attachment (Van IJzendoorn & Kroonenberg, 1988)				
Country	Type of attachment			Differences in child-rearing practices
	Secure	Avoidant	Resistant	
USA	65%	21%	14%	Mothers spend a great deal of time in close contact with the child.
WEST GERMANY	57%	35%	8%	Contact with mother but greater interpersonal distance between parents and child is the cultural norm. Independence is valued highly.
ISRAEL	64%	7%	29%	Children raised communally as part of kibbutz culture and so have no contact with strangers.
JAPAN	68%	5%	27%	Children very rarely separated from mother and so have little contact with strangers, so the Strange Situation is extremely stressful.

Description

Ψ Do the findings show any consistency?

Ψ What variation exists between individualistic and collectivist cultures?

Evaluation

Ψ Consistency suggests universality in attachments.

Ψ Variation within cultures is greater than variation between cultures.

Ψ Measurement of cross-cultural attachment is invalid as it uses a technique developed in one culture to study another culture—the Strange Situation is an imposed etic.

Conclusions

The significant v_____ in attachment w_____ cultures and the fact that the Strange Situation as a measure of attachments is c_____ b_____d mean that any conclusions about cultural variations in attachments lack v_____. The research is also limited because it is descriptive, not explanatory, as it does not tell us w_____ there is so much variation in at_____t within c_____.

Explanations of Attachment

For details, see Eysenck's textbook (pages 102–112) and Brody and Dwyer's revision guide (pages 48–51). Use the cues in the table to guide your note taking and fill in the gaps using the letter clues provided.

Learning theories
According to learning theories, attachment like all b_____ is s_____ by the en_____. Based on the behavioural explanations of c_____ conditioning and o_____ conditioning, attachment is a consequence of ass_____ and r_____. The emphasis is on the e_____, i.e., the external, as the explanation for attachment.

Ψ Classical conditioning—associating the mother with food.

Ψ Operant conditioning—the mother is a source of positive reinforcement.

Ψ Drive-reduction (Dollard & Miller, 1950).

Evaluation

Ψ How do Harlow's (1959) findings on the importance of 'contact comfort' contradict 'cupboard love'?

Ψ Learning theory is reductionist.

Social learning theories

This explanation is that attachment is learned through o_____ and i_____ of role models (e.g., the parents) and re_____. This requires some intervening m_____ p_____, which is not taken into account by traditional learning theories as they ignore the role of co_____.

Ψ Learn by observation and imitation.

Ψ Parents teach their children to love them and social skills through:
  • Modelling.

  • Direct instruction.

  • Social facilitation.

Evaluation

Ψ Has increased understanding of the role of interactional processes and so has some validity and practical applications.

Ψ Does not account for the emotional intensity of attachments.

Bowlby's theory

E_____ and p_____ theory influenced Bowlby's (1951) work. Thus, he supports ethology's claim that attachment is i_____ and must be formed within a c_____ p_____ (7 months–3 years), and that its main purpose is to promote s_____. As with psychodynamic theory, Bowlby suggested that attachment acts as a t_____ for all future relationships. He expanded on this with the concept of m_____, which means that attachments form a h_____ where the infant has one main attachment, and this is a special bond different from all other attachments.

Attachment is an adaptive process

Ψ Safety and survival—which theory is this based upon?

Ψ Innate: programmed to attach, and being a biological mechanism, it has a critical period (ends between 1 and 3 years). There is evidence that it is innate—what do babies imprint onto?

Ψ Internal working model—which theory is this based upon?

Ψ Monotropy: one special relationship.

Ψ Attachment is a psychological 'stay-close' mechanism where the mother is used as a secure base.

Ψ Attachment is reciprocal (two-way)—what role do 'social releasers' play?

Evaluation

Ψ How generalisable is the imprinting process to human attachments? Consider the skin-to-skin hypothesis (Klaus & Kennell, 1976).

Ψ Evidence for the internal working model: Hazan and Shaver's (1987) 'love quiz'.

Ψ The 'love quiz' research has weaknesses that limit it as supporting evidence.

Ψ Bowlby's theory was highly influential and inspired important further research such as the Strange Situation.

Ψ Not all attachments are hierarchical (Schaffer & Emerson, 1964) and so this contradicts monotropy.

Ψ The internal working model is deterministic. Not all relationships are the same as the primary attachment and even if they are, there are alternative explanations, which challenge the internal working model as a template.

Ψ Evolutionary theory is post-hoc and so cannot be tested.

Find out for yourself: Research the 'love quiz' online to measure your attachment type. Consider the weaknesses of this self-report survey.

Disruption of Attachment, Failure to Form Attachment (Privation), and Effects of Institutionalisation

For details, see Eysenck's textbook (pages 115–125) and Brody and Dwyer's revision guide (pages 54–59). Use the cues in the table to guide your note taking and fill in the gaps using the letter clues provided.

Bowlby's theory of a_____ predicted that s_____ attachment was needed for h_____ development. If this is valid then any disruption to the attachment process should result in u_____y p_____l development. Bowlby's m_____l d_____n hypothesis was revolutionary for the time (early 1950s) because at this point it was felt that adequate ph_____l provision was the most important determinant of h_____y development.

Short-term effects of deprivation
Robertson and Bowlby's (1952) PDD model • Protest.   • Despair.   • Detachment.   **Evaluation** Ψ Oversimplistic, as it does not account for individual differences.   Ψ Bond disruption may not occur.

Long-term effects of deprivation
The maternal deprivation hypothesis • Affectionless psychopathy. • Bowlby's (1944) 'forty-four juvenile thieves' study.

Institutionalisation and anaclitic depression

Bowlby's research is based on studies by:

Ψ Spitz and Wolf (1946).

Ψ Goldfarb (1947).

Evaluation

Ψ Deprived of stimulation and attention, not just maternal care.

Ψ Positive impact on hospital and institutional practices.

Ψ The concept of deprivation (Rutter, 1972).

Ψ Rutter criticised Bowlby for confusing causation with correlation. Maladjustment may be caused by other factors.

Ψ It is a product of the context—it suited the political agenda at the time.

Distinguishing separation, deprivation, and privation

Robertson and Robertson (1971) distinguished separation (no bond disruption) from deprivation (bond disruption). Rutter (1972) has criticised Bowlby's concept of deprivation as too general as it is used to account for d_____ types of early experience, which have quite different e_____. He distinguishes between d_____ and p_____. Rather than rejecting it, Rutter has redefined Bowlby's hypothesis. His research on adolescents living on the Isle of Wight led him to conclude that separation does not inevitably result in m_____ and delinquency. He found that family discord due to d_____ was four times more likely to lead to maladjustment than separation as a result of physical i_____ or d_____ of the mother. Thus, the reason for the separation, i.e., family discord, is more influential than the separation itself. This expands on the maternal deprivation hypothesis as o_____ f_____ involved in maladjustment have been identified. The family d_____ may have prevented b_____ from forming and so the adolescents experienced p_____, which is more likely to lead to d_____y than d_____. Rutter (1981) suggests that the effects of p _____ are much more s _____ and 1 _____ -1 _____ than the effects of d _____.

Long-term effects of privation

Hodges and Tizard's (1989) study of institutionalised children

Bowlby claimed the negative effects of deprivation could not be undone. Affectionless psychopathy was a permanent retardation of emotional development. This is deterministic as it suggests we have no control over our own behaviour.

Ψ Summarise the key procedures, findings, and conclusions of Hodges and Tizard's (1989) study into privation.

Ψ Hodges and Tizard's research reveals that the effects can be reversible and so can be used as a criticism of Bowlby.

Ψ The children's difficulties in relationships outside the foster home do support Bowlby's concept of an internal working model.

Case studies of privation

	Evaluation Ψ Adverse effects can be reversed.
Czech twins (Koluchová, 1976, 1991)	
Genie (Curtiss, 1989)	Ψ Methodological criticisms.
Children of the Holocaust (Freud & Dann, 1951)	

Research into the effects of institutionalisation

Ψ Rutter and the ERA Study Team (1998).

Ψ O'Connor et al. (2000).

Ψ Smyke et al. (2007).

Ψ Sigal et al. (2003).

Conclusions

Development is more flexible and less deterministic than the maternal d_____ h_____ suggests. As the research evidence is c_____ we must avoid drawing cause-and-effect conclusions. Other factors such as in_____ and si_____ differences contribute to the effects and this leads to multiple outcomes. Thus, m_____ is a possible but not inevitable consequence of maternal deprivation. The research evidence on the effects of i_____ and the more extreme case studies of pr_____ show that to some extent adverse e_____s can be reversed. This means that although children are more resilient than B_____y suggested, his hypothesis is not invalidated as there are long-term effects of privation for some more so than others.

Find out for yourself: Do an internet search of 'Victor, the wild boy of Aveyron' to find out about the earliest study of privation.

Using this in the exam: Attachment

You may be asked:

Short answer AO1 questions

1. Outline characteristics of secure or insecure attachment.
2. Outline the learning or evolutionary explanation of attachment formation.
3. Outline cultural variations in attachment.
4. Outline the effects of failure to form attachment.

Short answer AO2 questions

1. Explain how the evolutionary explanation of attachment differs from the behavioural explanation of attachment.
2. Evaluate the learning or evolutionary explanation of attachment formation.
3. Explain how disruption of attachment can have long-term effects.
4. Explain cultural variation in attachment.

Short answer AO3 questions

1. Explain why research lacks validity, e.g., studies of attachment, or privation.
2. Explain the ethical issues in research into the types of attachment.

Long answer questions

These can be either 8 marks or 12 marks, where AO1 : AO2 is 50 : 50 so be prepared to give a shorter or longer version of this answer depending on whether the question is 8 or 12 marks.

1. Outline and evaluate one explanation of attachment. (8 or 12 marks)

Paragraph 1 AO1 Outline the key features of Bowlby's theory.
Outline Bowlby's theory, including the fact it takes an evolutionary approach; attachment is innate and linked to survival, and so a biological process with a critical period. Also include the internal working model and monotropy.

Paragraph 2 AO2 Discuss strengths and weaknesses of the theory.
Evaluate Bowlby's theory: The claim that attachment is based on evolution (survival) accounts for the intensity of mother–child bonds. Include evolutionary criticisms—evolution is not a scientific theory; it is speculative because there is a lack of evidence, i.e., we cannot tell from fossils how they were attached, and so the theory has limited scientific validity. These limitations weaken Bowlby's theory as he draws heavily from evolution.

The determinism of the internal working model—what about the effects of later relationships? Later relationships are not just a product of the first attachment. This ignores the individual's free will to overcome a poor early attachment and so is deterministic and oversimplified (reductionist). Schaffer and Emerson (1964) provide evidence of multiple attachments, which may not be hierarchical and it is not always possible to identify which attachment is strongest, hence this contradicts monotropy. Monotropy may be valid for some but is not generalisable to all. Whilst Bowlby's theory has many negative criticisms, it has made important contributions to our understanding of attachments…

2. Discuss research into variations in attachment. (8 or 12 marks)

Paragraph 1 AO1 Describe the individual and cultural differences in attachments.

Outline individual and cross-cultural variations. Ainsworth and Bell's (1970) research on secure and insecure attachments, the temperament and maternal sensitivity hypotheses, and Van IJzendoorn and Kroonenberg (1988). You need link sentences such as 'Ainsworth's research shows that there are differences in attachment type…'; 'Research shows there are cross-cultural variations…'; 'This research supports the claim that there are variations…'.

Paragraph 2 AO2 Evaluate the research given in Paragraph 1.

Consider the criticisms of the research into variations in attachment as these weaken the evidence, e.g., reliability—is the measure of attachment reliable? Whilst there is evidence for (e.g., Main, Kaplan, & Cassidy, 1985) there is also evidence against, as children can have different attachment types with different caregivers, suggesting that this is not a stable variation (Main & Weston, 1981), and so we cannot be sure of the true nature of variations in attachment. Is the measure of attachment valid? The Strange Situation is an imposed etic and so ethnocentric (culture-biased). Why? This means measures of attachment in other cultures may not be valid and so we cannot be sure of the real nature of how attachments vary across cultures. Validity is a further issue because having only three attachment types is oversimplified (reductionist) as attachments may be impossible to classify into just three types. Main and Solomon (1986) have suggested type D (disorganised) because some infants cannot be categorised. The artificiality of the Strange Situation procedure may affect the validity of the attachment types. If we're not sure of validity then it's difficult to conclude if the attachment types are consistent (reliable) and true (valid) variations, and then there are also many universals! Yet it makes sense (face validity) that there are variations in attachments and these are probably best accounted for by the transactional model.

3. Outline and evaluate the effects of disruption of attachment including the effects of privation and institutionalisation.

Paragraph 1 AO1 and a little AO2 Outline the maternal deprivation hypothesis, give evidence for the effects of deprivation and privation, and give Rutter's criticism of the concept of deprivation.

Outline the maternal deprivation hypothesis, e.g., effects of deprivation as a consequence of separation. The disruption of attachment can lead to the breaking of the attachment bond and this can be permanent, as once broken the bond cannot be repaired and affectionless psychopathy may result. Bowlby's (1944) 'forty-four juvenile thieves' study provides evidence of the long-term effects of deprivation and privation. Use Rutter's criticism that Bowlby failed to distinguish between deprivation and privation…for example, some of the sample in Bowlby's '44 juvenile thieves' experienced deprivation and others privation. It can be predicted that privation would have more negative long-term effects; Hodges and Tizard (1989) provide some evidence for the effects of privation due to institutionalisation…

Paragraph 2 AO2 Discuss what the research suggests about the long-term effects.

Consider the weaknesses of Bowlby's research, e.g., it is correlational, and so other factors may be involved, as Clark and Clark (1976) suggest, and as Rutter's research on the Isle of Wight illustrates. Also, Bowlby's research may be biased and the case study method lacks generalisability. Thus, the findings may lack validity, and therefore meaning, and so may not be evidence of long-term effects. Hodges and Tizard's study and research on Romanian orphans show that the long-term effects of privation/institutionalisation can be reduced. This contradicts a critical period as institutionalised children did form attachments after the age of four years. Thus, a sensitive period rather than a critical period may be more accurate. Bowlby's (1956) research in the TB clinic showed that to some extent the effects of deprivation can be overcome. It demonstrates the importance of the substitute care in minimising bond disruption. Also, experiences in middle and later childhood are just as important as those in early childhood (Clarke & Clarke, 1976). Research does evidence long-term effects of deprivation/privation but it also evidences that some of these effects can be reversed. As Bowlby and others identified in the TB clinic, the effects depend on the amount of bond disruption, and as Tizard's research suggests, the quality of subsequent care. However, the research on effects is correlational and so other factors may be involved and in reality there are multiple outcomes, which also depend on characteristics of the individual, and situational factors.

Day Care

For details, see Eysenck's textbook (pages 127–133) and Brody and Dwyer's revision guide (pages 61–64). Fill in the gaps using the letter clues provided and use the cues in the table to guide your note taking.

This is a practical app_____ of psychological research on attachments because it raises the controversial issue of whether day care has negative effects on children's c_____ and s_____ development. There are arguments for and against d_____ c_____. The argument against is that any s_____ from the c_____ is harmful according to some interpretations of the m_____ d_____ hypothesis. The argument for is that day care benefits some children. For example, pre-school programmes such as O_____ Headstart were set up as a way of compensating for so_____ disadvantage. Thus it is important to consider that the effects of day care can vary due to i_____ d_____ and the type of d_____ c_____ experienced. The effects on s_____ development are of particular concern because day care has been linked to a_____ and p_____ relations.

Types of day care
Childminders
Ψ Mayall and Petrie (1983).
Ψ Bryant et al. (1980).
Day nurseries
Ψ Kagan et al.'s (1980) study that showed no difference between nursery and home care.
Ψ Vandell and Corasaniti (1990).
NICHD research
Research carried out by the National Institute of Child Health and Human Development (NICHD) is considered as high quality for the following reasons, and can be used to identify the limitations of other research.
Ψ It distinguishes between quality of care, quantity of care, and type of care.
Ψ The research is longitudinal.
Ψ The quality of parenting is considered.
Ψ The NICHD research distinguishes between five different types of day care.

Effects on peer relations

Positive effects

Ψ Day care may not affect the security of the child/caregiver attachment (Clarke-Stewart et al., 1994, and Roggman et al., 1994).

Ψ Sociability (Shea, 1981).

Ψ Advanced peer relations (Clarke-Stewart et al., 1994).

Negative effects

Ψ Some find it a threatening experience (Pennebaker et al., 1981).

Ψ Day care can have negative effects on the relationship between infant and caregiver:
  - Increased risk of insecure attachments (Belsky & Rovine, 1988).

  - It may damage the infant/caregiver relationship if it occurs before the age of 2 years (Sroufe, 1990).

The effects of day care may be neither positive nor negative

Ψ Day care has been found to have no significant effects on six measures of social development (Erel, Oberman, & Yirmiya, 2000).

Effects on aggression

Positive effects

Ψ Children may learn more effective ways of dealing with interpersonal conflict through time spent in day care.

Ψ Children in day care have been found to be less physically aggressive than those cared for full-time at home in one Canadian study (Borge et al., 2004).

Ψ Day care is associated with assertive behaviour—a positive effect (NICHD, 2003a, 2003b).

Negative effects

A number of studies have linked day care to aggression and behaviour problems:

Ψ Vandell and Corasaniti (1990).

Ψ Bates et al. (1994).

Ψ Belsky (1999).

Ψ The time spent in large groups has also been identified as a factor, which suggests larger day care centres may have more negative effects in terms of aggression (Haskins, 1985, and Schwartz et al., 1974).

Ψ Effects may be worse in centres involving large groups of peers than in other types of day care (Van IJzendoorn et al., 2004, and Belsky et al., 2007).

Evaluation

Ψ Association not causation is identified in day care research.

Ψ Research does not distinguish fully enough between the many factors involved, e.g., quantity and quality of day care, type of day care, quality of parenting etc.

Ψ Generalisability of research findings is an issue as children are not randomly assigned to the different types of day care, and so effects may be due to other factors than just the type of day care.

Ψ Insufficient longitudinal research has been conducted.

Ψ Due to children entering day care so early the research is retrospective not prospective and so it is not clear if the aggression is due to the day care or if it existed prior to the day care.

Ψ Effects depend on attachment type (Egeland & Hiester, 1995).

Ψ Effects determined by an interaction of quality of day care and maternal sensitivity.

Ψ The level of stimulation in the home environment.

Implications of Research into Attachment and Day Care for Child-Care Practices

For details, see Eysenck's textbook (pages 133–137) and Brody and Dwyer's revision guide (pages 64–67). Use the cues in the table to guide your note taking and fill in the gaps using the letter clues provided.

With so much governmental pressure on parents to return to work in addition to the economic pressure they face, it may be a mistake to see day care as a choice. Thus, it is important to establish what the effects of day care are and how we can ensure that they are positive. It appears that separation is not the key issue in respect to day care given that some children appear to benefit from day care. Thus, quality of care is the more relevant issue. How would you set about raising and maintaining high quality day care? Which type of day care would you recommend to concerned parents and why?

Features of high-quality day care
Ψ Sensitive emotional care.
Ψ Interaction and active engagement.
Ψ Consistency of care.
Ψ Relatives as caregivers and low aggression.
Ψ Low child-to-caregiver ratio.
Ψ Training.

Consistency of care	Quality of care
Ψ Lack of consistency (Tizard, 1979).	Ψ The amount of verbal interaction between caregiver and child.
Ψ High consistency (Kagan et al., 1980).	Ψ Stimulation.
	Ψ Sensitive emotional care.
Ψ The NICHD study (1997).	Ψ Howes et al.'s (1998) caregiver intervention programme.

Implications for child care practices

Ψ High quality care can compensate for insecure attachment.

Ψ Positive implications of day care for securely attached children (Belsky & Fearon, 2002; Wartner et al., 1994).

Ψ Attachment type at 12 months has long-term effects (Wartner et al., 1994).

Ψ Link between caregiver sensitivity and secure attachment has implications for training of child-care staff.

Ψ Child–environment fit—centre-based vs. child-care home or in-home care.

Ψ Relationship between group day care and level of social disadvantage (Borge et al., 2004).

Ψ A trade-off between negative effects and increased peer relationships needs to be considered.

Ψ Insecure attachment may be due to the parents' level of anxiety rather than the day care itself (Harrison & Ungerer, 2002).

Ψ Working parents may provide *benefits* rather than negative effects (Brown & Harris, 1978; Shaffer, 1993).

Conclusions

The c_____-to c_____ ratio and training of staff are important because more training and lower ratios lead to more: _____ between caregiver and child.

Effects vary depending on the q_____ of care, the t_____ of day care, the individual differences of the child and the caregiver, and the amount of st_____ in the h_____ environment. Hence, effects are subject to great v_____. As the evidence is c_____, cause and effect cannot be inferred as there are many factors involved in the association. Q_____ is perhaps the greatest determinant of whether e_____ are p_____ or n_____. What conclusions can you draw about the effects of day care?

Using this in the exam: Attachment in everyday life

You may be asked:

Short answer AO1 questions

1. Outline the effects of day care on aggression.
2. Outline the effects of day care on peer relations.

Short answer AO2 questions

1. Explain why day care may have positive effects on social development.
2. Explain why day care may have negative effects on social development.
3. Explain the implications of research into attachment and day care for child-care practices.
4. Explain how the effects of day care on social development may vary across different forms of day care.

Short answer AO3 questions

1. Explain why research lacks validity, e.g., research into the effects of day care.

Long answer questions

These can be either 8 marks or 12 marks, where AO1 : AO2 is 50 : 50 so be prepared to give a shorter or longer version of this answer depending on whether the question is 8 or 12 marks.

1. Outline and evaluate research into the effects of day care on social development (e.g., aggression, peer relations). (8 or 12 marks)

Paragraph 1 AO1 Outline evidence for day care having positive effects.

Identify different types of day care (nurseries, childminders, nannies, crèches) and explain how the effects on social development may vary depending on the type of day care. Outline evidence for the positive effects on social development. For example, research by Shea (1981), Clarke-Stewart et al. (1994), and Roggman et al. (1994) support the positive effects of day care on social development.

Paragraph 2 AO2 Contradict with evidence against and discuss criticisms of the research into day care.

Discuss the research evidence on the negative effects on social development. For example, Pennebaker et al., (1981), Belsky and Rovine (1988), and Sroufe (1990) contradict that day care has positive effects. Consider that effects are modified by individual differences in attachment type, the level of stimulation in the home environment, the type of day care, and the quality of day care, which must be taken into account when trying to 'weigh-up' for the conclusion. There are multiple outcomes of day care, which mean it is difficult to draw conclusions. Certainly the many variables mean that there is not a clear relationship between day care and effects on social development. Furthermore, as research is correlational then it cannot be concluded that day care causes effects on social development. But given the evidence that day care can be positive then the focus should be on transferring this to cases where day care still has negative effects. Thus, the good practice of high-quality day care needs to be identified: factors such as consistency of caregivers, low child : staff ratio, training of child-care staff, the number of interactions, and sensitivity of staff to the children in their care.

2. Discuss the implications of research into attachment and day care for child-care practices. (8 or 12 marks)

Paragraph 1 AO1 Outline the implications.

Outline the implications from research such as consistency of care and quality of care, and describe how the latter in particular has been linked to training. Also outline the study in Florida where the effects of higher caregiver to child ratios and training were manipulated (Howes, Smith, & Galinsky, 1995). Outline the implications from research on attachments as to how insecure and securely attached children respond to day care.

Paragraph 2 AO2 Evaluate the usefulness and limitations of the implications.

Evaluate the research in Florida; the fact that variables were manipulated means that cause and effect conclusions can be made. Also consider the value of the knowledge we have gained and the usefulness of the applications, for example, our understanding of maternal sensitivity has led to programmes to increase maternal sensitivity. The effects of day care are multiple and difficult to predict but conclude that it is important to consider the child–environment fit and explain why this may mean a child with aggressive tendencies is better in a home care environment than a centre-based environment. Discuss the implications of social background as, in the study by Borge et al. (2004), only those from very socially disadvantaged backgrounds did not increase in aggression in group day care. Evaluate that any negatives (and it is debatable whether aggression is negative as some argue this is a form of assertiveness) need to be balanced against the positives such as advanced peer relations. Also discuss the fact that the implications in terms of parental choice may be limited as parents may have little choice but to work, and it is important to recognise that there are benefits of the parent working for both the parent and the child (Brown & Harris, 1978).

Research Methods
Learning Objectives

The research methods questions will be contextualised within the other five topics in the examination and so the questions may be a slightly different format from the general types of questions in this chapter. However, an understanding of these general types of questions is needed before you can apply this knowledge in the exam, so do consider carefully the types of exam question that arise out of each area of Research Methods.

On completion of this topic you should be familiar with the following things.

Methods and techniques

- *Experiments*: laboratory, field, quasi, and natural experiments.
- *Correlational analysis*: the interpretation of correlation coefficients, i.e., direction (positive and negative) and strength 0 = no correlation to 1 = perfect correlation.
- *Observational techniques*: controlled and naturalistic; overt and covert; participant and non-participant.
- *Self-report techniques including questionnaire and interview*: open ended vs. closed questions; structured vs. unstructured interviews.
- *Case studies*: the in-depth study of an individual or small group.

Investigation design

- *Aims and hypotheses*: experimental (alternative), correlational, and other non-experimental hypotheses vs. the null hypothesis; directional vs. non-directional hypotheses.
- *Variables*: IV and DV (experimental), and V1 and V2 (correlational).
- *Experiment and research design*: independent measures (an experimental and control group; weakness participant variables), repeated measures (an experimental and control condition; weakness order effects), matched participants, and non-experimental research designs (e.g., naturalistic observation, interview, and questionnaire).
- *Factors associated with investigation design*: operationalisation (measurement of variables), pilot studies, demand characteristics and investigator effects, extraneous variables and bias, and how to control for these (e.g., random allocation, single/double blind procedures, standardisation, counterbalancing).
- *Samples and populations*: types of sampling (e.g., opportunity and random); the issue of generalisability.
- *Reliability and validity*: how to test for and improve reliability and validity.
- *BPS code of ethics and ethical issues*: Show awareness of the BPS guidelines, ethical issues, and ways in which psychologists deal with such issues.

Data analysis presentation and interpretation

- *Levels of measurement*: nominal, ordinal, interval, ratio.
- *Measures of central tendency*: mode, median, mean.
- *Measures of dispersion*: range and standard deviation.
- *Graphs and tables*: presentation, analysis, and interpretation of graphs (normal distribution, bar chart, histogram, frequency polygon, scattergram) and tables of data.
- *Correlational data*: presentation, analysis, and interpretation of correlational data including scattergrams, the direction of correlations (positive and negative) and interpretation of correlation coefficients (strength 0–1).
- *Content analysis*: making qualitative data quantitative through coding data into categories, also known as transcribing the data.
- *Discourse analysis*: analysis of words for patterns and themes.

Understand the following issues

- *Quantitative vs. qualitative methods*: advantages and weaknesses, which can be overcome to some extent by using a combined approach (called triangulation).
- *The scientific nature of psychology*: objectivity vs. subjectivity.

Cross-reference the above learning objectives with the Specification and fill in the self-assessment box below on completion of the topic.

SELF-ASSESSMENT BOX
☺ **Which of the above do you know?**
☹ **Are there any gaps in your knowledge that need to be targeted during revision?**

Research Methods

For details, see Eysenck's textbook (pages 141–164) and Brody and Dwyer's revision guide (pages 75–84). Fill in the gaps using the letter clues provided and use the cues to guide your note taking.

Research is the crux of psychology. In order to move beyond amateur and anecdotal explanations for behaviour we need research evidence to support the explanations or theories.

Research methods take either a qu_____ or qu_____ approach, which depends on whether the data collected is numerical or non-numerical. Thus, quantitative = n_____ and qualitative = w_____. Quantitative methods are concerned with objective m_____ and so try to quantify and describe b_____r. In contrast, qualitative methods are concerned with gaining ind_____ h data and so try to establish valid (true) ex_____for behaviour. All methods can be used in a scientific or non-scientific way, so do not make the mistake of seeing quantitative as the former and qualitative as the latter. Both approaches have strengths and weaknesses and so should be seen as equally valuable. It is optimal to combine the approaches and this is called tr_____n.

Advantages and weaknesses

Give two advantages and two weaknesses for each of the following methods.

Laboratory experiments
The laboratory experiment takes place in a controlled environment and enables the experimenter to test the effect of the IV (independent variable) on the DV (dependent variable). In order to establish a difference and so detect cause and effect relationships, the IV is systematically varied between two conditions.

Field experiments
Field experiments take place in natural settings, e.g., a work environment. The experimenter has control of the IV and so causal relationships can be established.

Quasi-experiments
Quasi-experiments exist when the experimenter cannot control the IV; it is said to be naturally occurring. For example, experiments involving gender, age, class, or cultural differences would all be classed as quasi-experiments because the experimenter cannot manipulate any of these as the IV. However, the experimenter does have control of the research setting.

Natural experiments
A natural experiment is a kind of quasi-experiment, but the researcher has no control over the IV or the research setting.

Correlational analysis

Correlational analysis is a technique that measures the strength of the relationship between two variables. The paired scores of the two variables are analysed to establish the strength and direction of the association, e.g., the relationship between stress and illness. This can be illustrated visually through scattergrams and numerically through correlation coefficients. These range from +1 to 0 to −1, where the sign shows the direction, and the number shows the strength of the association.

Observational techniques

Observation involves examining behaviour in a natural setting with minimal intrusion from the researcher as it aims to observe people's natural behaviour. Participants may be aware they are being observed (overt observation), or not (covert observation). Controlled observations are when the researcher has control of the environment in which the observation takes place.

Interviews

Interviews can take many different forms: non-directive, informal, guided, clinical, or structured. They usually take place face-to-face and can yield rich, in-depth data.

Questionnaires

Written questionnaires are a type of interview. They can be conducted face-to-face, via the telephone, or by post. They consist of a standard set of questions that are either closed (fixed-response, e.g., rating scales) or open-ended (which allow detailed responses). Questionnaires are used to survey attitudes, beliefs, and behaviour.

Case studies

The in-depth study of an individual or small group. Examples that you will come across during your AS studies include: case studies of abnormality, e.g., Little Albert and Anna O; case studies of brain damage, e.g., HM; and case studies of privation, e.g., Genie.

Using this in the exam

The above exercise will prepare you for exam questions that ask you to select a suitable method or give the advantages and disadvantages of a particular method.

Aims and Hypotheses

For details, see Eysenck's textbook (pages 167–169) and Brody and Dwyer's revision guide (page 84). Fill in the gaps using the letter clues provided and use the cues in the table to guide your note taking.

Aim: A general statement of why the study is being carried out

For example:

1. To investigate the effect of alcohol on perceived attractiveness of the opposite sex.
2. To investigate if women self-disclose more than men in a survey.
3. To investigate a gender difference in aggression.
4. To investigate the association between personality and self-esteem.
5. To investigate if chimps' behaviour does evidence a theory of mind.
6. To investigate the relationship between stress and illness.

See if you can decide whether the above aims would be tested as experimental, correlational, or non-experimental hypotheses. (Clue: there are two of each!)

Note the hypothesis number in the appropriate box below.

Hypothesis: A specific testable statement that predicts the expected outcome of the study

Alternative hypothesis for an experimental design (otherwise known as an experimental hypothesis)

An experimental hypothesis predicts a d_____ between two condition groups.

Alternative hypothesis for a non-experimental design

Non-experimental research, e.g., interviews and observations, may not be analysed quantitatively and so will not predict a difference or association. Instead, the hypothesis will predict what the researcher expects to o_____r or the th_____ (patterns of response) the researcher expects to discover.

Alternative hypothesis for a correlational design

A correlational hypothesis predicts an a_____n or r_____p between two variables. It is a special kind of non-experimental hypothesis. There is a _____ correlation between _____ and _____ = formula for correlational hypothesis. The sign is optional depending on whether the hypothesis is directional or not.

Directional and non-directional hypotheses

Hypotheses are either directional or non-directional. A directional hypothesis predicts the direction of the difference (experimental) or relationship (correlation), whereas a non-directional hypothesis predicts that there is a difference or relationship but not the direction of the difference or relationship.

Now see if you can write the examples as both non-directional (1–3) and directional (4–6) hypotheses.

Ψ 1.

Ψ 2.

Ψ 3.

Ψ 4.

Ψ 5.

Ψ 6.

Null hypothesis

Null hypothesis for an experimental design
Predicts n_ d_____ between the two condition groups. The IV has no effect on the DV, e.g., there will be no significant difference between X and Y and any differences that do exist are due to chance and/or random variables.

Null hypothesis for a correlational design
Predicts n_ r_____ between the two variables, e.g., there is no correlation between X and Y and any association that does exist is due to chance and/or random variables.

Null hypothesis for a non-experimental design
Predicts that the observed behaviour or pattern of response will not occur. Thus, transfers the statement into the negative.

Analysis of the results will reveal whether a significant difference or relationship does exist. If results prove significant the experimental or correlational hypothesis is a_____ and the null hypothesis is r_____.

Finally, write a null hypothesis for each of the examples.

Ψ 1.

Ψ 2.

Ψ 3.

Ψ 4.

Ψ 5.

Ψ 6.

Using this in the exam

Exam questions may ask you to state the aim or hypothesis based on the stimulus in the question. The hypothesis will usually be experimental or correlational (so ask yourself: is a difference or a relationship being investigated, and make sure you use the correct term). For example:

Suggest a suitable <u>aim/directional/non-directional/null hypothesis</u> for this investigation. (2 marks)

Note that the question above indicates the direction of the hypothesis. However, you could be asked to identify whether the hypothesis is directional or non-directional. For example:

State whether your hypothesis is directional or non-directional and justify your choice. (3 marks)

EXAM TIP: Where underlining occurs, only one of the terms would be given in the question.

Variables

For details, see Eysenck's textbook (page 169) and Brody and Dwyer's revision guide (pages 72 and 78).

Experimental variables

Experiments involve two variables: the IV (independent variable) and the DV (dependent variable). The experimenter *manipulates* the IV (or it varies naturally) and *measures* the DV. The IV has a specified effect on the DV and so changes in the IV will result in changes in the DV.

Correlational variables

Correlational investigations involve two co-variables V1 and V2. These co-variables are associated but because of the lack of control it cannot be ascertained if they are causally related.

The variables are specified in the hypothesis.

Following the example below, test your knowledge of hypotheses and variables by stating whether the following hypotheses are: 1) experimental or correlational, 2) directional or non-directional, and 3) identify either the IV and DV, or V1 and V2.

Delete the incorrect hypotheses and variables, and fill in the blanks. The first one is a completed example.

1. There is a gender difference in the percentage of conformity on Asch's line experiment.
   Alternative hypothesis: Experimental/~~Correlational~~   ~~Directional~~/Non-directional
   Variables:IV/~~V1~~= gender   DV/~~V1~~= percentage of conformity

2. There is a positive correlation between self-report measures of stress and anxiety.
   Alternative hypothesis: Experimental/Correlational   Directional/Non-directional
   Variables: IV/V1 =_____   DV/V2 =_____

3. Attachment type as measured by the Strange Situation varies between individualistic and collectivistic cultures.
   Alternative hypothesis: Experimental/Correlational   Directional/Non-directional
   Variables: IV/V1 =_____   DV/V2 =_____

4. Participants who use semantic processing will remember significantly more words from a previously memorised word list than those who use non-semantic processing.
   Alternative hypothesis: Experimental/Correlational   Directional/Non-directional
   Variables: IV/V1 =_____   DV/V2 =_____

5. There is a relationship between number of hours' sleep and self-report measures of mental alertness.
   Alternative hypothesis: Experimental/Correlational   Directional/Non-directional
   Variables: IV/V1 =_____   DV/V2 =_____

6. People with high authoritarian personality scores are significantly more obedient than people with low authoritarian personality scores.
   Alternative hypothesis: Experimental/Correlational   Directional/Non-directional
   Variables: IV/V1 =_____   DV/V2 =_____

7. There is an association between number of life events experienced and number of days' illness in previous 12 months.
   Alternative hypothesis: Experimental/Correlational   Directional/Non-directional
   Variables: IV/V1 =_____   DV/V2 =_____

8. Ratings of physical attractiveness of both members of a dating couple are associated.
   Alternative hypothesis: Experimental/Correlational   Directional/Non-directional
   Variables: IV/V1 =_____   DV/V2 =_____

Using this in the exam

Exam questions may ask you to identify the variables from the study described in the question stimulus. So know the difference between the IV and DV. For example:

What was the <u>independent variable/dependent variable</u> in this investigation?   (1 mark)

If the research is correlational make sure you do not identity the variables as IV and DV, but as co-variables, variable 1 and variable 2. You may also be asked to operationalise a variable so make sure you are familiar with different ways of measuring behavior (e.g., frequency, rating scale, time, etc., as appropriate).

Experimental Research Designs

For details, see Eysenck's textbook (pages 170–176) and Brody and Dwyer's revision guide (page 85). Fill in the gaps using the letter clues provided and use the cues in the table to guide your note taking.

The three designs aim to control participant variation, i.e., i_____ d_____ between the participants, which could interfere with the effect of the IV on the DV. All three designs share a common characteristic of experiments: two c_____, and the IV is varied across these. This usually involves a c_____l condition, which is not exposed to the IV and so acts as a baseline, and an e_____l condition, which is influenced by the IV and so shows the effect of this in comparison to the control condition.

Independent design		
Two groups of different participants. Thus, different participants in each of the conditions. Participants experience one condition.	**Strengths** Ψ Avoids order effects. Ψ Random allocation.	**Weaknesses** Ψ Participant variables. Ψ Number of participants.

Matched participants design		
Participants in each condition are matched on a one-to-one basis on certain relevant variables. Participants experience one condition. Thus, there are two groups, but they are matched, and each experiences a different condition.	**Strengths** Ψ Avoids order effects. Ψ Minimises participant variables.	**Weaknesses** Ψ Does not eliminate participant variables. Ψ Difficult to achieve a good match.

Repeated measures design		
Same participants in both conditions. There is one group of participants who take part in two conditions.	**Strengths** Ψ Minimises participant variables. Ψ Fewer participants are needed.	**Weaknesses** Ψ Order effects. Ψ Demand characteristics are easier to guess.

Using this in the exam

You need to be able to select an appropriate design. For example, if you wanted to test the effect of the make of football boots on performance, which design should be used?

Non-experimental Research Designs

Naturalistic observation

The following design factors need to be considered:

Ψ Overt or covert observation.

Ψ Participant or non-participant observation.

Ψ Event, time, and point sampling.

Ψ Recording the data, e.g., frequencies, observation criteria, notes, video or audio recordings.

Ψ Behavioural categories—the precision of these categories and the training of observers are of key importance.

Ψ Ethical considerations.

Interviews

The following design factors need to be considered:

Ψ Structured, semi-structured, or unstructured.

Ψ Constructing good questions.

Ψ Ethical considerations.

Questionnaires

The following design factors need to be considered:

Ψ Closed and open questions.

Ψ Ambiguity and bias.

Ψ Attitude scale construction.

Ψ Ethical considerations.

Using this in the exam

Any of the above designs could come up in the exam and you would also need to draw from the 'Factors associated with research design' worksheet if asked how to design an experiment, naturalistic observation, interview, or questionnaire.

Factors Associated with Research Design

For details, see Eysenck's textbook (pages 176–178 and 191–194) and Brody and Dwyer's revision guide (pages 89 and 90). Fill in the gaps using the letter clues provided and use the cues in the table to guide your note taking.

The following all need to be considered in the design of research to ensure that there are no serious flaws that will undermine the reliability and validity of the research. A lack of control can lead to: systematic or c_____ error, when one condition's experience is in some way different from the other's (e.g., one group tested in the morning and the other in the afternoon). OR un_____ or random error, when there is a lack of s_____ and participants' e_____ differ within and between conditions.

Operationalisation
In quantitative research the variables in the hypothesis must be defined precisely. That is, it must be clear how the variables will be measured. If the exam question asks you to operationalise the variables, explain how they can be measured.   Ψ Advantages of operationalisation.   Ψ Limitations of operationalisation.

Pilot study
This is a small-scale trial run of the main study.   Ψ Test materials.   Ψ Test procedure.

Control of experimental designs—the weaknesses of the designs are potential extraneous variables
Independent design   Participant variables are the weakness of this design and these are controlled by large samples and random allocation.
Repeated measures design   Order effects are the weakness of this design and these are controlled by counterbalancing, e.g., ABBA. OR randomisation is an alternative to counterbalancing.

Further extraneous variables and bias

Confounding variables interfere with the effect of the IV on the DV. The researcher cannot be confident that the change in the DV is due to the IV if extraneous variables are a source of constant error.

Ψ Situational variables.

Ψ Distraction and confusion.

The relationship between the researcher and participant

Ψ Demand characteristics and participant reactivity, e.g., evaluation apprehension, social desirability bias, the Hawthorne effect.

Ψ Investigator effects, e.g., experimenter expectancy.

Control of extraneous variables and bias

Standardisation is used to ensure that all of the participants experience the same research process. Variables must be controlled and deception may be needed to avoid participant reactivity and investigator effects.

Ψ Hold extraneous variables such as noise, temperature, and time of day constant.

Ψ Standardised instructions and procedures control for distraction and confusion, and participant reactivity and investigator effects. They also ensure research is replicable.

Control of participant reactivity and researcher effects

Ψ Single-blind procedure.

Ψ Double-blind procedure.

Using this in the exam

Identify two ways you could operationalise the IV in this study. (2 marks)

Explain what a pilot study is, why a pilot study should be conducted, and how you would carry this out. (2 + 2 + 2 marks)

Identify two potential extraneous variables in the context of this study. (2 marks)

Explain two features of the study that might affect the validity of the data being collected. (2 + 2 marks)

Explain one way in which the relationship between the researcher and participant might have influenced the results obtained in this study. (2 marks)

Describe one way that investigator effects (or participant reactivity) might threaten the validity of your study and suggest a way to overcome this. (3 marks)

Describe one way that demand characteristics might influence your findings. (2 marks)

Reliability and Validity

For details, see Eysenck's textbook (pages 178–181) and Brody and Dwyer's revision guide (pages 91–92)
Fill in the gaps using the letter clues provided and use the cues in the table to guide your note taking.

Reliability and validity are used to judge the quality of research.

Reliability	
Reliability is based on c_____. If the research produces the same results every time it is carried out then it is reliable. **Internal reliability = consistency within the method** Ψ Measuring instruments. Ψ Reliability of observations.	Internal and external reliability can be checked using c_____ t_____. **Techniques to check internal reliability** Ψ Split-half technique. Ψ Inter-rater reliability (or inter-judge reliability).
External reliability = consistency between uses of the method Ψ Reliability of psychological tests.	**Techniques to check external reliability** Ψ Test–retest reliability.

Validity

Campbell and Stanley (1966) have distinguished between i_____ and e_____ validity.

Internal validity = does it measure what it set out to? Is the effect genuine?	**External validity = g_____ to other settings (e_____) and populations**
Ψ Experimental validity—is the IV really responsible for the effect on the DV?	Ψ Coolican (1994) identifies four main aspects to external validity: • Populations.
Ψ Coolican (1994) identifies many threats to internal validity, i.e., other factors that could have caused the effect on the DV: • Confounding variables.	
• Unreliable measures.	• Locations.
• Standardisation.	
• Randomisation.	• Measures or constructs.
• Demand characteristics.	
• Participant reactivity.	• Times.
Ψ Good research design increases internal validity.	
Checking internal validity Ψ Replication.	**Checking external validity** Ψ Meta-analyses.

Using this in the exam

You may be asked to explain reliability or validity so make sure you can accurately distinguish between internal and external in terms of both reliability and validity.

The BPS Code of Ethics

For details, see Eysenck's textbook (pages 181–183 and Brody and Dwyer's revision guide (pages 92–94). Use the textbook to note down key points about each guideline.

Ethical guideline
Ψ Deception.
Ψ Informed consent.
Ψ Protection of participants.
Ψ Confidentiality.
Ψ Debrief.
Ψ Right to withdraw.

Ethical Issues and the Ways in Which Psychologists Deal with Them

For details, see Eysenck's textbook (pages 184–188) and Brody and Dwyer's revision guide (pages 95–97). Use the cues in the table to guide your note taking.

Ethical issues arise during the implementing of research. Ethical guidelines have consequently been introduced to set standards for the conduct of research. A cost–benefit analysis is used as a way of assessing the ethical issues as this involves weighing up if the ends justify the means.

Cost–benefit analysis	
The double-obligation dilemma Ψ Means: cost to participants. Ψ Ends: benefits to society.	**Evaluation** Ψ Difficult to predict outcomes (Diener & Crandall, 1978). Ψ Quantification is difficult. Ψ Researcher bias and value judgements— assessment depends on who is making the judgement. Ψ There is a bias in favour of society over participants. Ψ Decision is a moral dilemma, which is what the guidelines aimed to stop (Baumrind, 1975).

Why do ethical issues arise in psychological research?
Ψ Psychology involves the study of living creatures. Ψ Research findings may be 'socially sensitive'. Ψ Social control.

Key ethical issues

Ethical issue	Resolution
Ψ Deception.	Ψ Role play. Ψ Debrief.
Ψ Informed consent.	Ψ Presumptive consent. Ψ Prior general consent. Ψ Right to withhold data and retrospective consent.
Ψ Protection of participants. What is the key way to assess harm? Ψ Physical harm. Ψ Psychological harm.	Ψ Confidentiality. Ψ Right to withdraw. Ψ Debriefing.

Evaluation of the BPS ethical guidelines

The BPS code of ethics provides clear g_____ and so has helped reduce e_____ i_____. However, the code is not l_____ and so has l_____ force; the penalty disbarment from the BPS is not s_____ enough. Another issue is that breaches can be j_____ and that decisions as to whether research is justifiable can be r_____ b_____. This has led to the increasingly widespread development of ethical c_____s. Most institutions where research takes place (universities, research units, hospitals) have such committees, which means the decision as to whether the research is j_____ is less b_____d than if just the researcher makes it. However, ethical committees are not without b____, most are sat upon by psychologists, who may be biased in favour of r_____, and so it is optimal if the committee also consist of non-p_____ and non-expert members of the p_____.

Sampling

For details, see Eysenck's textbook (pages 188–191) and Brody and Dwyer's revision guide (pages 97–99). Fill in the gaps using the letter clues provided and use the cues in the table to guide your note taking.

Research is conducted on people, and the group of people that the researcher is interested in is called the target p_____. However, it is usually not possible to use all of the people from here and so a s_____ must be selected. Those selected are called p_____ for research purposes.

Thus, research is conducted on a sample but the researcher hopes that the findings will be true (valid) for the target population. For this to happen the sample must be r_____ of the target population. If the sample is representative then the findings can be g_____ back to the target population. If not, the findings lack population v_____. Therefore, the key issue is the generalisability of the sample, and this is based on two key factors:

Ψ *Type* of sampling.   Ψ *Size* of the sample.

Random sampling
Ψ Random methods—every participant has an equal chance of being selected.
Evaluation
Opportunity sampling
Ψ Availability.
Evaluation
Volunteer sampling
Ψ Self-selected.
Evaluation
Sample size
There is no ideal number of participants, but a number of factors must be considered: Ψ   Ψ   Ψ   Ψ   **Golden rule**

Using this in the exam

You could be asked to identify a method of sampling and to explain how you would implement it. Random sampling is the easiest way to ensure you access all of the marks, as you need to explain that this means 'every participant has an equal chance of being chosen' and then explain how to do this, e.g., random number table, or names out of a hat.

Suggest a suitable method for selecting participants and explain how you would carry this out.   (1 + 2 marks)

Quantitative Analysis of Data

See Eysenck's textbook (pages 197–202) and Brody and Dwyer's revision guide (pages 103–106). Follow the instructions in the table and practise the calculations.

Descriptive statistical techniques summarise the data. Measures of central tendency and dispersion are descriptive statistics. The findings can also be summarised using graphs. However, to decide which is the appropriate measure or graph to use, the level of measurement must first be established.

Level of measurement listed in order of increasing precision (note the acronym: NOIR)
Nominal: **O**rdinal: **I**nterval: **R**atio:
Measures of central tendency
You may have heard of the three measures before; they are averages, and so involve the calculation of a single number representative of the other numbers it is associated with. The average is the central point in the score distribution.
MODE—the number that occurs most frequently.   **Advantage:** Quick and easy to calculate and can be used whatever the level of data.   **Limitations:** This is not widely used in psychological research as it is subject to great variability and provides very limited information. It does not tell us about the other values in the score distribution. A further problem is that it is possible to have more than one modal value; two modal values are known as **bimodal values**, and more than two are called **multi-modal**.   Calculate the mode in the example below.   E.g., 2 4 5 5 6 6 6 7 8 10
MEDIAN—the **middle value** when the scores are arranged from lowest to highest. Half the values in a score distribution are above the median, and half below it. When there is an even number of scores the two middle values are added together and then divided by two.   **Advantages:** Can be used when you are unsure about the **reliability** of the extreme values and when you have **skewed distributions**. It can be used with **ordinal** or **interval** levels of measurement.   **Limitations:** The median is susceptible to minor alterations (variability) in the data set (score distribution).   Calculate the median in the example below.   E.g., 2 4 5 5 6 6 6 7 8 10
MEAN—this is the arithmetic average. To calculate, add all the values together and divide the total by the number of values.   **Advantages:** This is the best measure to use as it makes use of all the data in the score distribution.   **Limitations:** It is fine when the data forms a normal distribution (remember the bell-shaped curve) but when there are extreme outlying values (anomalies) the mean value is easily distorted and so the median should be used instead. The mean should only be used for data of interval or ratio measurement.   Calculate the mean in the example below.   E.g., 2 4 5 5 6 6 6 7 8 10

Measures of dispersion

These measure the variability within the data distribution, i.e., are the scores similar to each other or different? Thus, they are a measure of the spread of the scores in the data distribution.

Variation ratio—This complements the mode; it is the proportion of non-modal scores.

E.g., 2 3 6 6 6 7 7 8 8 10
Mode = 6

Proportion of non-modal scores = 7/10 × 100
So variation ratio = 70

Advantages: It is easy to calculate.
Limitations: This has the same key disadvantage as the mode; it is not representative of all scores in the distribution and so tends not to be used.
Calculate the variation ratio in the example below.
E.g., 1 3 3 4 6 6 7 7 7 7 8 9 9 9 10

Range—This is the difference between the highest and lowest scores in a data set.

1 is added if the scores are all whole numbers.
0.5 is added if values are recorded to the nearest half.
0.1 is added if the values are recorded to one decimal place.

Advantages: It is easy to calculate.

Limitations: The two most extreme values are used to calculate the range, so if these are outlying, the calculated range will not be representative of the distribution. It does not make use of all the data in the score distribution.

Calculate the range in the example below.
E.g., 1 3 3 4 6 6 7 7 7 7 8 9 9 9 10

Interquartile range—This solves the problem of outlying values as only the middle 50% of scores are used in the calculation. It also gives a better idea of the distribution of values around the centre.

Calculate the interquartile range in the example below.
E.g., 1 3 3 4 6 6 7 7 7 7 8 9 9 9 10

Standard deviation—This is a measure of variability, which measures scores in terms of difference from the mean.

Advantages: As with the mean, the standard deviation uses all the scores in a set of data and so is the best measure of dispersion to use. We can make inferences based on the relationship between the standard deviation and a normal distribution curve.

Limitations: It needs interval or ratio levels of measurement, and data to be approximately normally distributed.

Calculate the standard deviation in the example below.
E.g., 1 3 3 4 6 6 7 7 7 7 8 9 9 9 10

1. Calculate the mean.
2. Obtain the value of d (difference) by taking away the mean from each score.
3. Square all of the values of d and get the sum total of all of the values of d squared.
4. Divide this result by one less than the number of participants to get the variance.
5. Calculate s (standard deviation) by taking the square root of the variance.

Graphs and Charts

For details, see Eysenck's textbook (pages 202–205) and Brody and Dwyer's revision guide (pages 100–102). Use the cues in the table to guide your note taking.

Graphs and charts present the data visually. They are a useful way of summarising information as the data is easily accessible in a visual format.

Graphs and tables

Histograms

Ψ Sketch an example of a histogram.

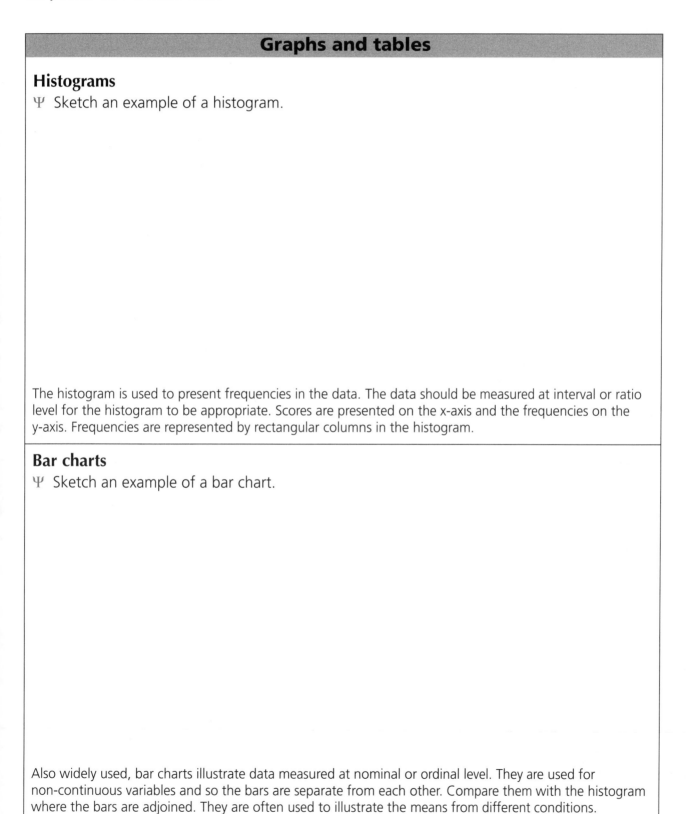

The histogram is used to present frequencies in the data. The data should be measured at interval or ratio level for the histogram to be appropriate. Scores are presented on the x-axis and the frequencies on the y-axis. Frequencies are represented by rectangular columns in the histogram.

Bar charts

Ψ Sketch an example of a bar chart.

Also widely used, bar charts illustrate data measured at nominal or ordinal level. They are used for non-continuous variables and so the bars are separate from each other. Compare them with the histogram where the bars are adjoined. They are often used to illustrate the means from different conditions.

Scattergraphs

Ψ Sketch an example of a scattergraph.

| Positive correlation | No correlation | Negative correlation |

Scattergraphs are used to present correlated data. It does not matter which variable goes on which axis. Correlations range from perfect positive (+1), to no correlation, to perfect negative (−1). The sign indicates the direction, and the correlation coefficient (the number) indicates the strength of the correlation. If scores are positively correlated they increase together. If they are negatively correlated, as the scores on one variable increase the scores on the other variable decrease. Perfect positive and perfect negative correlations are rare in psychological research. Imperfect correlations are more common, for example, +0.7 is an imperfect positive correlation and −0.4 is an imperfect negative correlation. The closer the correlation coefficient is to 1, the stronger the correlation. You must be able to interpret the direction and strength of a correlation, so remember as a rule of thumb that low numbers 0.1–0.3 are weak correlations, 0.4–0.6 moderate, and 0.7–1 strong (although it is a little more complex than this as strength depends on the size of the sample). Also remember the weaknesses of correlational data when making interpretations, i.e., be able to explain how lack of cause and effect and the role of other factors limit conclusions.

Tables

Ψ Sketch an example of a table.

A table can be an effective way of summarising a large amount of data, for example, measures of central tendency and dispersion can be provided in one table. It has the advantage of being very precise, e.g., figures are readily apparent, whereas graphs may only allow approximate figures to be worked out. However tables can be harder to interpret than graphs as it is more difficult to visualise the data.

Qualitative Analysis of Data

For details, see Eysenck's textbook (pages 205–209) and Brody and Dwyer's revision guide (pages 107–109). Use the cues in the table to guide your note taking.

Qualitative data can be collected via naturalistic observation, interviews, and questionnaires.

Data can take many forms:

Ψ

Ψ

Ψ

Thus, the data is words, not numbers, and the emphasis is on meaning.

Principles of qualitative analysis
Ψ Gather data.
Ψ Consider categories suggested by participants.
Ψ Analyse the meanings, attitudes, and interpretations, e.g., DISCOURSE ANALYSIS.
Ψ Consider the research hypothesis and possibly how it has changed as a result of the investigation.
Ψ Making qualitative data quantitative, e.g., CONTENT ANALYSIS.
Evaluation

Using this in the exam

You may be asked to interpret any of the graphs on the previous page in the exam. So make sure you are clear on how to interpret them. You may be tested on which graph you would select to represent data, so read the uses of each graph again so you know when each graph is most appropriate. You could also be asked to select an appropriate qualitative or quantitative method of analysis and to explain how you would carry this out.

Identify a suitable graph or chart that could be used to illustrate the data in Table 1 and give one reason why this would be an appropriate descriptive method.   (1 + 1 marks)

State one or two conclusions that can be drawn from the data in Figure 1/Table 1 and use this data to explain your answer.   (2 marks or 4 marks)

Describe an appropriate method for analysing the data, why this is an appropriate method, and how you would put this into practice.   (2 + 2 + 2 marks)

Research Methods Revision

Use this as a checklist and tick off as you feel confident you can answer the different types of question.

Types of exam question

Ψ The Method question

For example: Identify the research method used in this investigation and explain one advantage and one disadvantage of this method. (1 + 2 + 2 marks)

You need to be able to identify the method being used from the question and give advantages and disadvantages of this method. So can you give two advantages and two disadvantages for each method?

Please remember that not all research is experimental. It may be wisest if you refer to all research as 'the study' so as not to make the mistake of calling a non-experimental method 'the experiment'.

Ψ The Research Design question

For example: Identify the research design used in this investigation and explain one advantage and one disadvantage of this design. (1 + 2 + 2 marks)

Describe the aims and procedures of a possible follow-up study (or of this study). (6 marks)

Any of the research designs could come up and you would also need to draw from the 'Factors associated with research design' worksheet.

Know the difference between independent measures (two different groups of participants), repeated measures (one group of participants who experience both conditions), and matched participants (same as independent but the participants are matched). Know the advantages and disadvantages, e.g., participant variables and order effects, and know the controls for these (see random allocation and counterbalancing questions). Also, know how to implement and evaluate the non-experimental research designs. The aims/procedures question is particularly important as there are 6 marks for this question, so draw from 'Research methods'.

Ψ The Aims/Hypothesis question

For example: Describe an aim/directional hypothesis/non-directional/null hypothesis of this investigation. (2 marks per question)

Can you give an experimental (significant difference) hypothesis, a correlational (significant correlation/ relationship) hypothesis, and a null hypothesis? Decide whether the hypothesis is directional or nondirectional and justify your choice, i.e., refer to previous research.

Ψ The Operationalisation question

For example: Identify two ways in which you could operationalise… (2 marks)

How can the variables be measured, e.g., frequencies (nominal), rating scale (ordinal)? You need to be able to explain the operations, e.g., operationalise risk-taking behaviour.

Ψ The Variable question

For example: Identify the IV or DV, or both, in this investigation. (1 mark or 2 marks)

Experimental: The IV is the variable manipulated or controlled by the experimenter, or naturally occurring (e.g., age, gender, culture). The DV is the variable that is measured to show the effect of the IV. Don't describe what an IV or DV is as I have done here. Instead use this information to help you identify the variables from the question stimulus.

Correlational: V1 and V2. It does not matter which variable is 1 or 2 so just identify the two co-variables that are associated.

Ψ The Investigator Effects question

For example: Describe one way that investigator effects might threaten the validity of your study. (2 marks)

Researcher-bias when setting the research question (formulation), in the carrying out of the research (e.g., giving away the demand characteristics and the researcher expectancy effect), in the analysis of the results (manipulation of the data), and in the interpretation of the data.

Ψ The Participant Reactivity question

For example: Describe one way that participant reactivity might threaten the validity of your study. (2 marks)

This occurs when participants respond to the demand characteristics, which are cues in the research situation, or given away by the researcher, that might reveal the research hypothesis.

Participant reactivity includes the co-operative participant who tries to guess the research hypothesis in order to comply with it, or the negativistic participant who tries to guess the research hypothesis in order to work against it. Participants may also show evaluation apprehension, which can lead to the social desirability effect, or the Hawthorne effect, that is, participants' behaviour changes as a consequence of being researched.

Ψ How to Control Investigator Effects/Participant Reactivity question

For example: Explain one way to overcome investigator effects/participant reactivity. (2 marks per question)

Single-blind procedure controls for participant reactivity, as this is where the hypothesis is withheld from the participant and so they are not aware which condition they are in. This reduces demand characteristics.

Double-blind procedure controls for researcher expectancy as this involves a research assistant who collects the data without any knowledge of the research hypothesis. Thus, neither the researcher nor the participants know the research hypothesis and so the expectancy effect is controlled.

Ψ The Confounding Variables question

For example: Explain two features of the study that might have affected the validity of the data being collected. (2 + 2 marks)

If the question asks you to identify confounding variables, ask yourself what other variables could have affected the DV other than the IV? Will it have a systematic or unsystematic effect?

Participant variables: Give an example of an individual difference that is relevant to the study described in the question.

Situational variables: Give an example of an environmental difference that is relevant to the study described in the question.

Ψ The Standardisation question

For example: Explain one way to control for confounding variables. (2 marks)

Standardised procedures and instructions are used to ensure the research conditions are the same for all participants. This avoids some participants being treated more favourably than others, or some participants being given more demand characteristics than others, or some participants experiencing more distraction and confusion than others.

Ψ The Pilot Study question

☐

For example: Explain what a pilot study is, why a pilot study should be conducted, and how you would carry this out. (2 + 2 + 2 marks)

A pilot study is carried out to trial run the materials and procedure to identify any flaws or areas for improvement that can then be corrected before the main study, e.g., clarity of instructions, ambiguity of questions, timing, clarity of the procedure.

Ψ The Sample question

☐

For example: Suggest a suitable method for selecting participants and explain how you would carry this out and why it is an appropriate method for this investigation. (1 + 2 + 2 marks)

Which sample would you use? Why? And how?

Random sampling would be used because every participant in the target population has an equal chance of being chosen. Therefore it is less biased and is considered more representative of the target population. Use random number tables, a computer that generates random numbers, or names out of a hat to achieve a random sample.

Opportunity sampling is when you sample whoever is available. The fact that it is left to the researcher's discretion to approach whoever is available leaves room for bias as the researcher may sample people on the basis that they find them attractive or think they look approachable.

Ψ The Random Allocation question

☐

For example: Explain how you would control for the weaknesses of the independent measures design. (2 marks)

This refers to how the participants are allocated to conditions in the independent measured design. As with the random sample it is best if every participant has an equal chance of being allocated to the condition. This reduces bias and minimises participant variables, but does NOT eliminate them.

Ψ The Counterbalancing question

☐

For example: Explain how you would control for the weaknesses of the repeated measures design. (2 marks)

This refers to how the participants are allocated to conditions in the repeated measures design. It controls for order effects such as guessing the demand characteristics, practice, or fatigue, which may occur if all participants experience the two conditions in the same order. The ABBA design controls for this because half experience A then B and the other half experience B then A. This balances out the order effects across the two conditions but does NOT eliminate them.

Ψ The Validity question

☐

For example: Identify one way in which you could ensure validity and explain how you would put this into practice. (3 marks)

The external validity might be affected, i.e., the results may not generalise to other settings (ecological validity), people (population validity), or periods in time (temporal validity). Internal validity, i.e., did you measure what you claimed to? Researcher effects, participant reactivity, confounding variables, and experimental realism all decrease validity because the observed effect may be due to one of these and not the IV. Check for validity: replicate with different populations or in different contexts, e.g., replication and meta-analysis.

Ψ The Reliability question ☐

For example: Identify one way in which you could ensure reliability and explain how you
would put this into practice.   (3 marks)

Consistency within the research is internal reliability, and between uses of the measure is external reliability,
e.g., over time.

Check for reliability: replicate to see if the results are consistent over time, test–retest, or check that there is
consistency between two observers, inter-observer reliability/inter-rater reliability.

Ψ The Data Analysis question ☐

For example: Describe an appropriate method for analysing the data, why this is an
appropriate method, and how you would put this into practice.   (2 + 2 + 2 marks)

Identify a suitable graph or chart that could be used to illustrate the data in Table 1 and
give one reason why this would be an appropriate descriptive method.   (1 + 1 marks)

State one or two conclusions that can be drawn from the data in Figure 1/Table 1 and
use this data to explain your answer.   (2 or 4 marks)

Quantitative analysis—measures of central tendency and dispersion: know how to interpret the average
and the spread of the score distribution. Also know levels of measurement (nominal, ordinal, interval,
ratio). Practise interpreting graphs and tables and make sure you can select appropriate graphs and charts,
e.g., a scattergraph for correlated data, or a bar chart for discontinuous data.

Qualitative analysis—the stimulus study may be investigating meanings and so a qualitative analysis is more
appropriate. Make sure you know the principle of qualitative analysis and can describe how to carry out
discourse analysis and content analysis.

Ψ The Quantitative vs. Qualitative Approach question ☐

For example: Give an advantage and a disadvantage of the quantitative/
qualitative approach.   (2 + 2 marks per question)

Give advantages and disadvantages for each. For example, quantitative is scientific and so it is replicable
and therefore has high reliability, but it is descriptive and tends to lack validity. Qualitative gathers in-depth
data that is high in validity but is difficult to replicate and so lacks reliability.

Ψ The Ethics question ☐

For example: Identify one (or two) ethical issues that might have arisen
in this investigation, and explain how the researcher might have dealt with
them.   2 + 2 marks or 4 + 4 marks)

Identify two ethical issues. State which guidelines have been broken and why it is an issue in relation to the
study in the question. Similarly, if asked to give two ethical considerations state two guidelines and why
they should be observed. Be careful you do not state that you need informed consent when the hypothesis
has been deliberately withheld. Deception, informed consent, and protection of participants are the main
guidelines to consider.

Stress Learning Objectives

On completion of this topic you should be familiar with the following.

Stress as a bodily response

* Outline the body's response to stress including the sympathomedullary pathway (SAM), and the hypothalamic-pituitary-adrenocortical axis (HPA).
* Evaluate the physiological response to stress.
* Critically consider the relationship between stress and physical illness, in particular the effect of stress on the immune system.

Stress in everyday life

* Identify and analyse sources of stress, including life changes, daily hassles, and workplace stress.
* Discuss the personality factors that modify the effects of stress, including Type A behaviour.
* Distinguish between emotion-focused and problem-focused approaches to coping with stress.
* Critically consider psychological and physiological methods of stress management, including Cognitive Behavioural Therapy and drugs.

Cross-reference the above learning objectives with the Specification and fill in the self-assessment box below on completion of the topic.

SELF-ASSESSMENT BOX

☺ **Which of the above do you know?**

☹ **Are there any gaps in your knowledge that need to be targeted during revision?**

The Body's Response to Stressors

For details, see Eysenck's textbook (pages 213–219) and Brody and Dwyer's revision guide (pages 113–117).

Definition of stress

Imagine that you are experiencing a stressful situation, e.g., making a speech in front of a large audience, taking a driving test, or sitting an examination. What changes happen within your body when you are stressed? Read about the role of the autonomic nervous system and summarise what happens by filling in the blanks in the diagram below making sure you have included the following terms:

Hypothalamus	Pituitary gland	Corticosteroids
Adrenaline	Adrenal medulla	ACTH
Adrenal cortex	Noradrenaline	Sympathetic branch of the ANS

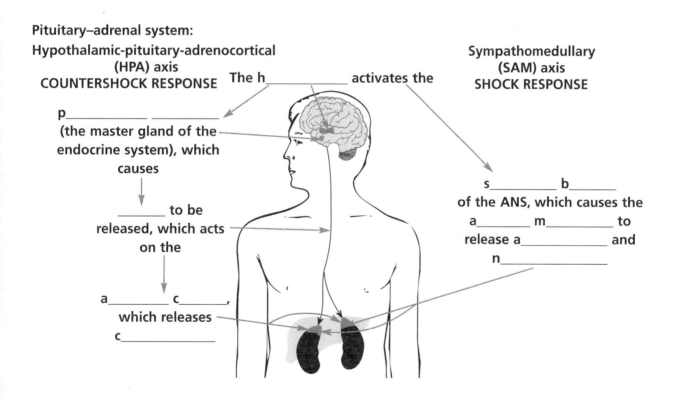

Pituitary–adrenal system:
Hypothalamic-pituitary-adrenocortical (HPA) axis
COUNTERSHOCK RESPONSE

The h_____ activates the

Sympathomedullary (SAM) axis
SHOCK RESPONSE

p_____ _____
(the master gland of the endocrine system), which causes

_____ to be released, which acts on the

a_____ c_____,
which releases
c_____

s_____ b_____
of the ANS, which causes the
a_____ m_____ to
release a_____ and
n_____

Now add onto the diagram the effects of 1) the immediate 'fight or flight' response due to arousal of the sympathetic branch of the ANS (the sympathomedullary axis), e.g., faster breathing and pulse, etc., and 2) the longer term stress response of the hypothalamic-pituitary-adrenocortical axis, e.g., release of cortisol, etc.

Evaluation of the HPA	Evaluation of the SAM

Stress-related Illness and the Immune System

For details, see Eysenck's textbook (pages 221–230) and Brody and Dwyer (pages 118–122). Fill in the gaps using the letter clues provided and use the cues in the table to guide your note taking.

There are two ways in which stress can cause illness:
Ψ Directly:
Ψ Indirectly:

Curtis (2000) has linked stress with a range of physical illnesses including, h_____s, inf_____ i_____, car_____ d_____, di_____, a_____a, and r_____d a_____s.

Stress and the immune system
Ψ Direct effects—stress decreases the number of white blood cells, known as immunosuppression.

Research evidence for immune suppression
Ψ Immunosuppression and cancer in mice (Riley, 1981).
Ψ Research into the effect of death of a spouse (Schliefer et al., 1983, and Segerstrom & Miller, 2004).
Ψ Exam stress and natural killer cell activity (Kiecolt-Glaser et al., 1984).
Ψ The effect of caregiving on the immune system (Kiecolt-Glaser et al., 1995).
Ψ Further evidence stress impairs wound healing (Marucha, Kiecolt-Glaser, & Favagehi,1998).
Ψ It is important to distinguish between the effects of stress on natural and specific immunity (Segerstrom & Miller, 2004).

Evaluation of the relationship between stress and immune suppression

Ψ There is strong evidence that supports the link between stress and immune suppression.

Ψ Practical applications.

Ψ The research only shows associations from which we cannot infer cause and effect and where other factors may be involved.

Ψ Evidence is inconclusive (Bachen, Cohen, & Marsland, 1997).

Ψ Functioning of the immune system of stressed individuals falls within the normal range.

Ψ Measurements of stress and the immune system may lack reliability and validity as the immune system is very complex and so difficult to assess.

Ψ Ignores individual differences.

Ψ Ignores psychological factors.

Conclusions

There is strong e_____ that links stress to illness. However, most of this evidence is based on natural e_____ or it is c_____al evidence. Consequently, c_____ and e_____ cannot be inferred: we cannot say that stress causes illness but can only say that it is a_____d with illness. Another methodological weakness of this research is the likelihood that o_____ f_____ are involved, such as l_____e, i_____ differences, and coping ability. Thus, individuals with a less stressful personality type (e.g., Type B or hardy personality) may be less v_____ to stress-related illness. To conclude, the relationship between s_____ and i_____ is highly complex and so caution should be taken when considering the direct effect of stress on illness. The stress response is not just physiological and so it is oversimplistic and red_____ to consider the relationship between stress and illness as purely physical. There are important ps_____ factors that mediate in this relationship.

Using this in the exam: Stress as a bodily response

You may be asked:

Short answer AO1 questions

1. Recognise the two pathways of the body's response to stress as presented in a stimulus question.
2. Outline the two pathways of the body's response to stress.
3. Outline the effects of stress on the immune system.

Short answer AO2 questions

1. Explain how stress affects the immune system.
2. Explain how stress affects the body.

Short answer AO3 questions

1. Give a methodological criticism of research into stress-related illness and the immune system.
2. Assess the validity of research into stress-related illness and the immune system.

Long answer questions

These can be either 8 marks or 12 marks, where AO1 : AO2 is 50 : 50 so be prepared to give a shorter or longer version of this answer depending on whether the question is 8 or 12 marks.

1. Outline and evaluate the body's response to stress. (8 or 12 marks)

Paragraph 1 AO1 Outline the body's response to stress.

Outline the body's response to stress, the dual-stress response (i.e., the SAM and HPA).

Paragraph 2 AO2 Evaluate the physiological response.

Research such as Selye's and our understanding of the body's response to stress has had positive implications in terms of our understanding of stress and illness. However, evidence against the usefulness of this research is that psychological factors that are also involved are ignored, e.g., self-perception. Research into the body's response to stress such as the GAS, e.g., extrapolation from rats and it is not a non-specific response as we do not respond in the same way to all stressors, i.e., different stressors have different effects. Also, individual differences modify the effects of stress and so show that it is not solely a physiological response, e.g., individual differences in self-perception, gender, personality, culture, and stress management. Research evidence is based on natural experiments and correlations and so cause and effect cannot be inferred as the IV has not been controlled. Thus, whilst the effects of stress on the body are incontrovertible, conclusive findings are difficult as in real life more than two variables are involved in such a complex response. The physiological response is indisputable but it only accounts for nature not nurture. This is only one level of the stress experience, which also occurs on a behavioural, cognitive, unconscious, and emotional level.

2. Discuss research into stress-related illness and the immune system. (8 or 12 marks)

Paragraph 1 AO1 Explain the link between the body's response to stress and immune suppression, and outline evidence for this link.

Explain how the HPA (immunosuppression) has been linked to stress and immune suppression. Give evidence for a relationship between stress and the immune system, such as Riley's research and the work of Kiecolt-Glaser et al.

Paragraph 2 AO2 Evaluate the research evidence.

The research has provided useful insights into the pathways between stress and illness, and the measures of immune response are objective and scientific. However, it is difficult to measure the functioning of the immune system and so it's difficult to assess this because it is very complex. Measures of immune functioning change depending on the type of stressor, duration, and timing, thus, the assessments that have been made in research, such as the number of white blood cells, may be over simplistic and so lack reliability and validity. Immune responses often fall within the normal range and so it is not clear how changes in the immune system increase susceptibility to diseases if the functioning of stressed individuals is within the normal range! Furthermore, the research ignores psychological factors and individual differences, i.e., self-perception, gender, culture, personality, stress management. Research is correlational so not a causal relationship; other factors may be involved and so it lacks explanatory power. The research is also based on self-report and this has problems of participant reactivity and response set—explain these. The research is also biologically reductionist and deterministic—again explain. Whilst stress is associated with illness, stress at all of the different levels (cognitive, emotional, behavioural) must be accounted for.

Sources of Stress

For details, see Eysenck's textbook (pages 232–241) and Brody and Dwyer's revision guide (pages 123–128). Fill in the gaps using the letter clues provided and use the cues in the table to guide your note taking.

Sources of stress are factors that c_____ stress. You need to know about l_____ ch_____, daily hassles, and wo_____ s_____ for the exam (which is another source of stress!). Holmes and Rahe (1967) were two doctors who noticed that their patients often experienced several l_____ c_____ prior to i_____.

Life events—Holmes and Rahe (1967)
Ψ Changes absorb 'psychic energy'.
Ψ Social Readjustment Rating Scale (SRRS)—43 life events.
Ψ A weak correlation between life change units (LCUs) and illness.

Evaluation of the SRRS evidence
Ψ Evidence is correlational.
Ψ There are individual differences in self-perception of the events. The SRRS fails to consider the context and subjective interpretations.
Ψ The SRRS does not distinguish between desirable and undesirable life events.
Ψ Self-report method is retrospective and may be biased by participant reactivity.
Ψ We lack understanding of how specific life events are associated with particular forms of illness.
Ψ Daily hassles are more representative of real-life stress (DeLongis et al., 1982).

Find out for yourself: Find Holmes and Rahe's SRRS online and complete the scale to find your LCU. Consider why it is a limited measure of stress. Give reasons why we cannot infer cause and effect from the statistically significant correlation between life events and illness.

Daily hassles

Ψ Types of daily hassles (Almeida, 2005).

Ψ A comparison of life events and daily hassles as a predictor of stress and health (DeLongis et al., 1982).

Ψ Limitations of the study by DeLongis et al. (1982).

Ψ How do daily hassles affect physical health? Use findings from Sher (2004) and Twisk et al. (1999).

Evaluation of daily hassles

Ψ In real life, daily hassles interact with life events and so combined effects should be considered (Johnson & Sherman, 1997).

Ψ Correlational criticisms.

Ψ Role of individual differences.

Ψ There is confusion between daily hassles and chronic (long-lasting) stressors (Hahn & Smith, 1999).

Workplace stress

Ψ Workplace stress in a Swedish saw mill (Johansson et al., 1978).

Ψ Burnout—an extreme stress response!

Ψ Major workplace stressors (Warr, 1996).

Ψ Predictability and controllability—a curvilinear relationship.

Ψ Marmot et al.'s (1997) 'hierarchy and control in the civil service'.

Ψ Weaknesses of Marmot et al.'s research.
  - Investigator effects and participant reactivity.
  - Correlational criticisms.
  - There were other differences besides job control.

Ψ Internal/external locus of control (Rotter, 1966). How can this be linked to workplace stress?

Ψ Effort–reward inbalance.

Personality Factors and Stress

For details, see Eysenck's textbook (pages 241–247) and Brody and Dwyer's revision guide (pages 128–130). Fill in the gaps using the letter clues provided and use the cues in the table to guide your note taking.

Failing to account for p_____ f_____ is a key criticism of the approach to physiological s_____. The identification of T_____A/B p_____ as a psychological factor in the relationship between s_____ and i_____ was a major break through in our understanding of stress.

Personality
Ψ Personality types: A, B, C (Friedman & Rosenman, 1959):   • Type As.   • Type Bs.   Ψ Friedman and Rosenman's (1974) Western Collaborative Group Study.   **Evaluation of Friedman and Rosenman's study**   Ψ Usefulness and implications of the research.   Ψ Oversimplification of the Type A/B classification.   Ψ Correlational criticisms.   Ψ Lack of precision of which aspects of Type A personality correlate with coronary heart disease (Matthews et al., 1997 and Ganster et al., 1991).   Ψ Applications of the research (De Leon et al., 1986).   Ψ The relationship is becoming weaker over time—maybe it was never that strong.

Find out for yourself: Find Friedman and Rosenman's Type A/B questionaire online and complete the scale to find your personality type. Consider why it is a limited measure of stressful personality type.

Hardiness

Ψ Kobasa (1979) suggests 'hardy' individuals are better able to cope with stress because of certain characteristics (remember the three Cs):

- Commitment:

- Challenge:

- Control:

Ψ Hardiness may have direct effects on stress and illness.

Ψ Hardiness may act as a buffer.

Evidence

Ψ Kobasa et al.'s (1985) study on male business executives.

Ψ Hardiness helps individuals cope with life events (Crowley, Hayslip, & Hobdy, 2003).

Ψ Hardy individuals employ different coping strategies from non-hardy individuals (Gentry & Kobasa, 1984).

Evaluation

Ψ Application—training programmes (Khoshaba & Maddi, 2001).

Ψ There is a range of evidence for hardiness.

Ψ The challenge component lacks relevance.

Ψ Sample bias as most studies involved male participants only, therefore there is an a_____ bias.

Ψ Neuroticism may have more of an effect than hardiness.

Ψ Correlational criticisms.

Emotion-focused and Problem-focused Approaches to Coping with Stress

For details, see Eysenck's textbook (pages 248–251) and Brody and Dwyer's revision guide (pages 132 and 133). Fill in the gaps using the letter clues provided and use the cues in the table to guide your note taking.

'Coping strategies' refers to any attempts to r_____ stress. This may involve taking a_____ to deal with the stressor (problem-focused) or it may be an attempt to reduce the negative e_____ caused by stress (emotion-focused) (Lazarus & Folkman, 1984).

Problem-focused	Emotion-focused
Ψ Examples of problem-focused coping strategies:	Ψ Examples of emotion-focused coping strategies:

So which strategy is more effective?
Ψ The main-effects hypothesis.
Ψ The goodness-of-fit hypothesis.
Ψ Folkman et al. (1986) suggest problem-focused is better.
Ψ Strategies may need to change as the stressful situation can change over time (Folkman & Lazarus, 1985).
Ψ Emotion-focused, e.g., denial, can be dangerous (Levine et al., 1987).
Ψ The use of coping strategies in response to life events supports the goodness-of-fit hypothesis (Forsythe & Compas, 1987).

Evaluation

Ψ The two general strategies account for a wide variety of specific coping strategies across a wide range of situations.

Ψ There are other types of coping not accounted for by these two approaches.

Ψ They are not completely separate approaches (Skinner et al., 2003).

Ψ Participants choose which strategies they employ and so findings may be due to personality factors.

Ψ Self-report criticisms: It may be just that and so it may not be a valid account of real-life behaviour and the self-report is too broad an assessment of coping.

Stress Management

For details, see Eysenck's textbook (pages 251–257) and Brody and Dwyer's revision guide (pages 134–137). Fill in the gaps using the letter clues provided and use the cues in the table to guide your note taking.

Stress m_____ is an important application given the incidence of stress-related i_____ in contemporary society. It is estimated that people have 10+ days of stress-related illness off per year! How do you c_____ when you're stressed? One of the key aspects of stress management is increasing one's s_____-e_____, that is increasing one's sense of c_____l. The definition of stress clarifies this as it shows that to decrease stress we must match our p_____n of c_____ a_____ to our perception of the de_____ of the s_____.

Psychological methods

Stress inoculation training (Meichenbaum, 1977, 1985)

There are three main phases to stress inoculation training (SIT), which should be introduced before the individual becomes too anxious or depressed. Remember the initials ASA to cue your recall. SIT takes a cognitive-behavioural approach, which means this technique aims to reduce stress by changing faulty cognitions and maladaptive behaviour.

Ψ Assessment.

Ψ Stress reduction techniques.

Ψ Application and follow-through.

Research evidence

Ψ Meichenbaum's (1977) comparison of SIT with systematic desensitisation.

Ψ Research into the effect of SIT on cortisol (Antoni et al., 2000 and Cruess et al., 1999).

Ψ The effect of SIT on healthy participants exposed to a brief stressor (Gaab et al., 2003).

Ψ Comparisons of SIT to prolonged exposure (Foa et al., 1999 and Lee et al., 2002).

Evaluation

Ψ It is effective because it increases sense of control and self-efficacy.
  - It is of similar effectiveness as other therapies.

  - It is effective with many types of stress.

  - Self-report and more objective cortisol measures provide evidence of SIT's effectiveness.

  - It has positive applications as training can be introduced.

Ψ It is not clear which components of the technique provide the most benefit.

Ψ Comparisons of SIT against no treatment lack validity.

Ψ In comparison to other forms of treatment SIT is generally less effective.

Ψ The 'therapy effect' may reduce stress rather than the SIT technique itself.

Ψ Individual differences in ability to use the technique.

Ψ Less effective in highly stressful situations.

Ψ It is less invasive than physiological techniques.

Ψ It may treat the causes better than physiological techniques.

Ψ Effectiveness of any treatment requires belief in the technique and some may lack belief in cognitive-behavioural techniques.

Physiological methods

Anti-anxiety drugs
Drugs work by controlling the body's response to stress either by acting on the sympathetic nervous system or on the stress hormones.

Ψ Beta-blockers
- How do they work?

Evaluation
Ψ Findings.

Ψ Side effects and issues of dependency.

Ψ A strength is that they have less effect on cognitive functions than benzodiazepines.

Ψ Benzodiazepines
- How do they work?

Evaluation
Ψ Fast acting.

Ψ They can be used with few side-effects over a short-term period.

Ψ Sedative side-effect.

Ψ Dependence and tolerance (drug escalation).

Ψ Long-term use can lead to permanent cognitive impairments (Stewart, 2005).

Ψ But are the impairments due to the drugs or individual differences in the people who use drugs compared to controls who do not?

Ψ Buspirone
- How does it work?

Evaluation
Ψ Findings.

Ψ No sedative effect.

Ψ Typically no withdrawal symptoms.

Ψ Doesn't impair cognition.

Ψ Does have some side-effects.

General evaluation
Ψ Can be highly effective.

Ψ Treat symptoms not causes.

Ψ Severe side effects of some, particularly benzodiazepines, have led to the recommendation that they be used for a restricted time only—how long is this?

Using this in the exam: Stress in everyday life

You may be asked:

Short answer AO1 questions

1. Outline factors that affect responses to stress e.g., life changes, workplace stress.
2. Outline personality factors in the body's response to stress.
3. Outline a physiological approach to stress management.
4. Outline a psychological approach to stress management.
5. Recognise characteristics of Type A and B personality as presented in the question stimulus.
6. Recognise life changes and daily hassles as presented in the question stimulus.

Short answer AO2 questions

1. Explain differences between emotion-focused and problem-focused approaches to coping with stress.
2. Explain differences between psychological and physiological methods of stress management.

Short answer AO3 questions

1. Give a methodological issue in assessing the effectiveness of methods of stress management.
2. Assess the validity of research into either: life changes, daily hassles, workplace stress, or personality factors.

Long answer questions

These can be either 8 marks or 12 marks, where AO1 : AO2 is 50 : 50 so be prepared to give a shorter or longer version of this answer depending on whether the question is 8 or 12 marks.

1. Discuss the use of drugs to manage the negative effects of stress. (8 or 12 marks)

Paragraph 1 AO1 Outline the key features of the stress management technique.

Physiological approaches to stress are techniques that try to control the body's response to stress by reducing physiological reactivity. Explain how barbiturates, benzodiazepines and buspirone are used to reduce the body's response to stress.

Paragraph 2 AO2 Discuss strengths and weaknesses.

However, there are issues of dependence (physical and psychological), tolerance, and side-effects—compare the different techniques. These drugs are effective in relieving the unpleasant physiological effects of stress because they are fast-acting compared to psychological techniques. Consequently, they are useful short-term strategies, which enable the individual to achieve a state where psychological intervention can be introduced. A key criticism of the physiological approach is that it ignores other factors, e.g., psychological factors in the stress response, such as underlying emotions and cognitions. The importance of psychological factors is illustrated by the fact that individual differences can modify the effectiveness of stress management techniques—use examples of personality differences and the importance of cognition to illustrate this. The fact that underlying factors are ignored leads to the criticism that drugs treat the symptoms but not the causes of stress—explain.

2. Discuss the use of Cognitive Behavioural Therapy to manage the negative effects of stress. (8 or 12 marks)

Paragraph 1 AO1 Outline the key features of the stress management technique.

Outline stress inoculation training (SIT)—Meichenbaum: Assessment, stress-reduction techniques, applications. Explain the approach SIT takes to stress management, i.e., targeting faulty cognitions and maladaptive behaviour. Research evidence by Antoni et al. (2000), Cruess et al. (1999), and Gaab et al. (2003) supports the effectiveness of the technique—outline their findings.

Paragraph 2 AO2 Discuss strengths and weaknesses.

Evaluate these techniques. The evidence suggests SIT is effective with many types of stress and so has useful applications. Consider how well SIT compares to other treatments and the fact that comparisons against no treatment lack validity. A key strength is that it addresses cognition and so may be treating the underlying causes, which will alleviate the symptoms. They are non-invasive (Why? Explain.) and so unlikely to have side-effects, although patients can initially feel unhappy when they confront their problems. But SIT requires self-insight because the patient must be able to assess/focus and this can be time-consuming. Effects may not be felt for some time and so require perseverance and patience. SIT does not work for everybody, the technique requires the patient to have belief in the effectiveness and some may question if they can change their cognition. Lack of motivation can lead patients to opt out of the treatment if they find the technique too difficult. SIT combines cognitive and behavioural principles, which is more effective because more than one level is being targeted. The techniques do increase control and self-efficacy, however this may explain any positive effect rather than the technique itself.

Social Influence Learning Objectives

On completion of this topic you should be familiar with the following.

Social influence

- Outline two explanations of majority influence, informational influence, and normative influence (Deutsch & Gerard, 1955).
- Describe the three kinds of conformity: compliance, identification, and internalisation (Kelman, 1958).
- Describe Milgram's (1963) 'electric shock experiment' and evaluate.
- Assess the internal validity and external validity of Milgram's research.
- Outline explanations of obedience, e.g., agentic shift and the authoritarian personality.

Social influence in everyday life

- Outline explanations of independent behaviour, including how people resist pressures to conform and pressures to obey authority.
- Discuss the infuence of individual differences on independent behaviour including locus of control.
- Critically consider implications for social change of research into social influence.

Cross-reference the above learning objectives with the Specification and fill in the self-assessment box below on completion of the topic.

SELF-ASSESSMENT BOX

☺ **Which of the above do you know?**

☹ **Are there any gaps in your knowledge that need to be targeted during revision?**

Majority Influence

For details, see Eysenck's textbook (pages 264–270) and Brody and Dwyer's revision guide (pages 141–143). Fill in the gaps using the letter clues provided and use the cues in the table to guide your note taking.

Majority influence or c_____ is a form of s_____ i_____ where we want to be liked by other people and so in part it is our desire to b_____g or fit in. Consequently, we experience gr_____ pr_____ to conform to the n_____ of the majority.

Definition of majority influence (conformity)

Explanations of conformity (Deutsch & Gerard, 1955)	
N_____e influence	I_____l influence

Types of conformity (Kelman, 1958)		
Compliance Ψ Change your b_____ but not your m_____.	**Identification** Ψ Change your b_____ to fit in with the g_____.	**Internalisation** Ψ Change your m_____ and b_____.

Factors that influence conformity	
Culture (Smith & Bond, 1993) Ψ Individualistic vs. collectivistic cultures.	**Historical context (Perrin & Spencer,1980)** Ψ The Asch effect was a 'c_____ of its t____'.

Types and Explanations of Conformity

For details see Eysenck's textbook (pages 270–282) and Brody and Dwyer's revision guide (pages 143–146). Use the cues in the table to guide your note taking and fill in the gaps using the letter clues provided.

Compliance and normative influence	
Summarise Asch's (1951) study and explain why it is an example of NORMATIVE INFLUENCE and the type of conformity is COMPLIANCE.	**Evaluate** • Era-dependence. • The study used strangers as the majority. • Lacks explanatory power—doesn't explain WHY… • Ethical issues.

Compliance versus internalisation

Summarise Kelman's (1958) research findings that support the distinction between compliance (normative influence) and internalisation (informational influence).

Identification and both normative and informational influence

Summarise Zimbardo's (1973) study and explain why it is an example of NORMATIVE and INFORMATIONAL INFLUENCE and the type of conformity is IDENTIFICATION.	**Evaluate** • Lack of mundane realism. • Participant reactivity.

Conclusions

Deutsch and Gerard (1955) predicted that in everyday life both n_____ and i_____ influence are at work together rather than just one or the other. Normative influence can be greatly reduced when participants' answers in the Asch paradigm are a_____ or when they have s_____ s_____. Informational is reduced when the situation is clear and the participant can be confident in their o_____ k_____. A weakness of normative influence shown by research where c_____ is highest to f_____ shows that normative is about g_____ belongingness not simply s_____ approval. Furthermore, these explanations only account for situational factors and so i_____ factors (e.g., personality, i_____) have been largely ignored, probably because personal factors are much harder to test e_____.

Obedience

For details, see Eysenck's textbook (pages 282–284 and pages 289–293) and Brody and Dwyer's revision guide (pages 149–151). Use the cues in the table to guide your note taking.

Obedience is when we do what we are told. Is this on the decline? Discuss.

Definition of obedience to authority

Explanations of obedience	
Agentic state—a situational factor	Authoritarian personality— a personal factor

Milgram's (1963) research into obedience	
Summarise the study:	Evaluation
	Ψ Importance of Milgram's findings.
	Ψ He does not explain why 35% of participants were disobedient.
	Ψ Ethical issues.

Find out for yourself: Conduct an observational study in your school/college of obedience. Decide how you will issue an 'order' and vary this across two conditions, e.g., presence and absence of an authority figure. Then measure the amount of obedience and disobedience to see if there is a difference between the two conditions. How will you measure this? What level of data will you obtain? How can you assess if there is a difference in the data? Consider the ethical and methodological issues raised by the study. Ensure that any request that is made is reasonable and one that would be made in everyday life.

Methodological Criticisms of Milgram's Research

For details, see Eysenck's textbook (pages 285–289) and Brody and Dwyer's revision guide (pages 151 and 152). Use the cues in the table to guide your note taking.

Orne and Holland (1968) have criticised the validity of Milgram's research. What is meant by the term 'validity'? There are two types of validity (see below).

Definition of internal validity

Definition of external validity

Example task

Your task is to draw a line to match up the following statements with the correct term that appears on the right-hand side. More than one term may apply. Identify whether the research in the statement HAS or LACKS the term you match it to. For example:

The experimental design did the job it set out to do. ←——— HAS ———→ **Internal validity**

The participants couldn't have believed in the set-up.   **Mundane realism**

The study can be applied to other settings.

Obedience is a demand characteristic.   **Internal validity**

Artificial laboratory research may not be representative of real life.

The participants showed signs of real distress.   **Experimental realism**

An experiment is a social situation and so a reflection of life.

Milgram's research has been successfully replicated in more   **External validity**
natural situations.

Ψ So what does this mean in terms of validity and realism?

Internal validity

Evidence for experimental realism
Ψ Evidence provided by Milgram, e.g., video tapes.

Ψ Participants' reactions.

Evidence against experimental realism
Ψ Demand characteristics.

External validity

Evidence for external validity
Ψ Milgram claimed his research had mundane realism.

Ψ Milgram's variation in a run-down office.

Ψ Cross-cultural replications.

Ψ Further studies, e.g., Hofling et al. (1966) and Bickman (1974).

Ψ Generalisability to the Nazi atrocities of the Holocaust.

Evidence against external validity

Ψ Lacks mundane realism.

Ψ Limited generalisability to current setting.

Ψ The external validity of the further studies can be questioned.

Conclusions

There are persuasive arg_____ for and against the v_____ of Milgram's research. His research has many w_____. However, the findings are still important as the research participants' belief that they were delivering el_____ shocks supports e_____ r_____m and so i_____ v_____y. Furthermore, the findings illustrated the fundamental attribution error, which is the tendency to u_____ the role of s_____ factors and o_____ the role of p_____ factors. Milgram's conclusion that the situational context was highly influential has been applied to the atrocities of the H_____, which demonstrates the gen_____ and thus e_____l v_____y of the research.

However, Milgram exaggerated the relevance of his r_____ to the Holocaust because the social processes that explain the Holocaust are much more complex than b_____ o_____. In conclusion, the processes of obedience shown in Milgram's study such as the role of the authority figure and the agentic state do seem to be true (internal validity) and representative of real-life obedience (external validity) to some extent, which is why Milgram's research has made such a significant contribution to our understanding of h_____ b_____. However, the fact that not all participants obeyed and that many of those that did showed extreme t_____n shows that it is not as simple as the participants being in an a_____c state; they clearly were still wrestling with their conscience rather than simply passing r_____y to the experimenter!

In real life people do not take f_____ responsibility for their actions as the experimenter did in the study! This does question the external validity of Milgram's research, and implies that situational factors are not the only influence. The fact that 35% did not obey shows the situational factors did not influence all participants in the same way. So rather than simply concluding that the situation explains obedience, we should consider further the individual differences that lead some to obey and others to disobey. The individual differences are more complex than merely whether participants had an a_____ personality or not because the majority of Milgram's participants did obey, yet far fewer than 65% had an a_____ personality.

Using this in the exam: Social influence

You may be asked:

Short answer AO1 questions

1. Outline types of conformity.
2. Outline explanations of conformity.
3. Outline research into obedience.
4. Outline explanations of obedience.

Short answer AO2 questions

1. Explain why you might obey in a given situation described in the stimulus material.
2. Explain why you might conform in a given situation described in the stimulus material.

Short answer AO3 questions

1. Assess the validity of research into obedience.
2. Discuss one ethical issue raised by research into obedience.

Long answer questions

These can be either 8 marks or 12 marks, where AO1: AO2 is 50 : 50 so be prepared to give a shorter or longer version of this answer depending on whether the question is 8 or 12 marks.

1. Consider whether criticisms of the validity of obedience research are justified. (8 or 12 marks)

Paragraph 1 AO1 Outline the criticisms of the validity and explain why they have been made.

Explain why Orne and Holland (1968) have criticised the validity of obedience research. Explain that the external validity of Milgram's research i.e., generalisability beyond the research setting, was questioned by Orne and Holland (1968) because of the lack of mundane realism and the power of the institutional context. The internal validity has been criticised, as Orne and Holland claimed that the experimental set-up was not believable and so lacked experimental realism—explain why. For example, Orne and Holland claimed that demand characteristics were evident in the experiment e.g., the shocks were not believable as disproportionate and these cues led the participants to role-play obedience and so the research lacked experimental realism.

Paragraph 2 AO2 Contradict the criticisms with evidence for the validity.

Evidence to support external validity is Milgram's variation in a run-down office building where 48% obedience was found rather than the 65% of the original study. Why does this support external validity? Smith and Bond (1993) provide cross-cultural support for ecological validity as findings were consistent with Milgram's in many other cultures. External validity is further supported by attempts to replicate the research e.g., Hofling et al. (1966) and Bickman (1974)—don't describe the research in detail, just give the findings and conclusions that support external validity. Give Milgram's defence of the internal validity, e.g., film evidence and debriefing (participants admitted they were deceived and rated the shocks as 15 on a scale of how painful they were (1 low–15 high). Milgram claimed the participants were genuinely deceived and so this supports internal validity.

2. Discuss what Milgram's research has to tell us about why people display obedience and why they may display resistance to obedience. (8 or 12 marks)

Paragraph 1 AO1 Outline explanations of obedience and resistance.

Milgram's research has provided key insights into explanations of obedience, such as the role of the authority figure...(ELABORATE) and the agentic state...(ELABORATE). It has also provided situational explanations of resistance to obedience such as increasing the consequences of the obedience, i.e., learner's distress, or decreasing the status of the authority figure. Both factors can decrease obedience and so increase resistance. For example, when the buffer of the wall was removed in later replications this led to resistance because...The disobedient role-model and giving orders by telephone increased resistance because...

Paragraph 2 AO2 Give positive and negative evaluations of the usefulness of the explanations.

An evaluation can be made that Milgram's research has contributed significantly to our understanding of obedience because Milgram's rejection of the `German's are different' hypothesis radically changed post-WWII views on destructive obedience. Prior to his findings, the accepted view was that obedience was a consequence of personality and that destructive obedience indicated a deviant personality, such as Adorno et al.'s (1950) authoritarian personality. Milgram's research suggested that situtuaional factors are more important and so that everybody has the potential to show blind obedience in the right circumstances; and similarly that the situational factors can increase resistance to obedience. Thus, Milgram's research illustrated the `fundamental attribution error' i.e., overemphasis on personal factors and underemphasis on situational factors, and so did provide a better understanding of why people obey. It also had positive implications because it showed that the Germans as a nation were not in some way deviant and so helped to decrease stereotyping and prejudice. Furthermore, his findings that resistance can be increased clearly have useful social implications as we can train people to resist obedience when they are uncomfortable with the consequences. However, the methodological weaknesses of the research question the usefulness of the insights because the research findings may lack truth. Provide Orne and Holland's (1968) arguments that demand characteristics limit internal validity and mundane realism, the institutional context, and the time and context of when the research was conducted limit external validty. Consider Milgram's claim that the lack of mundane realism (as clearly it wasn't like real life) may be made up by the high experimental realism (i.e., the research set-up was believable). Thus, it may be concluded that Milgram's research does offer valid insights into obedience and resistance to obedience. But the `obedience alibi' these situational explanations provide should not be accepted uncritically as he provides no independent evidence for the validity of the agentic state other than paritcipants' own statements, which of course could be biased by demand characteristics. The situational explanations of resistance offer only a partial understanding because there are also individual differences, which have not been researched as fully, probably because of the difficulty in testing individual factors.

Situational Explanations of How People Resist Pressures to Obey Authority and Resist Pressures to Conform

For details, see Eysenck's textbook (pages 296–298) and Brody and Dwyer's revision guide (pages 156–158). Use the cues in the table to guide your note taking.

Resistance to obedience

Milgram (1974) carried out many variations of his original remote-victim experiment. Two factors increased resistance to obedience. In the box below, write down the obedience percentages for each variation to see how much obedience reduced and resistance increased. Also, write down some details about the different variations. What is your comparison percentage (i.e., Milgram's original finding)?

Reducing the influence of the experimenter
Ψ Location of the experiment = _____ %
Ψ Orders by telephone = _____ %
Ψ A disobedient role-model = _____ %

Increasing the obviousness of the learner's distress
Ψ Voice feedback = _____ %
Ψ Proximity—1 metre away = _____ %
Ψ Touch-proximity—hand on shockplate = _____ %

Social support
Use the disobedient role model replication and the research by Rank and Jacobsen (1997, see Eysenck's textbook page 288) to explain the effect of social support on resistance.

Methods to develop resistance to obedience

Ψ E_____ people about the problems of 'b_____ o_____'.
Ψ Remind people that they should take r_____ for their own a_____. What would this prevent?
Ψ Provide r_____ m_____ who refuse to o_____.
Ψ Question the motives of a_____ figures when they issue u_____ orders.

Resistance to conformity

It has been used as a criticism that Asch's study is more an example of independent behaviour i.e., r_____ to c_____. 37% was the average c_____ rate, then _____% resisted conformity, and 26% of participants did not c_____ at all. Of course this criticism ignores the very unambiguous nature of the study, which made the c_____ that was shown highly significant.

Factors identified by Asch (1951, 1956) as decreasing conformity

Ψ Social support.

Ψ A small majority.

Ψ We conform more with who we know and so show resistance to strangers.

Ψ Culture.

Ψ Public vs. private conformity (see Eysenck's textbook pages 278–280).

Conclusions

The above are s_____ explanations of resistance to o_____ and c_____ because they refer to aspects of the research s_____ that led to a decrease in obedience or conformity. These are not the only factors that increase r_____ as characteristics of the i_____ also affect how susceptible they are to social i_____.

The Influence of Individual Differences on Independent Behaviour

For details see Eysenck's textbook (pages 298–303) and Brody and Dwyer's revision guide (pages 158–160). Use the cues in the table to guide your note taking.

Individual differences in obedience and conformity	
Ψ Individuals who protested at an early stage in obedience research (Modigliani & Rochat, 1995).	Ψ The effect of intelligence on conformity (see Eysenck's textbook page 281).

Attribution theory
Ψ Internal and external attributions in obedience research.
Ψ Internal and external attributions in conformity research.

Locus of control
Ψ Rotter's (1966) internal and external locus of control scale.
Ψ How does locus of control affect independent behaviour in the Asch and Milgram situations? Which factors are the externals more influenced by than internals?

Evidence

Ψ Research evidence for internals showing more independence on conformity tasks (Shute, 1975; London & Lim, 1964; Avtgis, 1998).

Ψ Research evidence against locus of control affecting conformity (Williams & Warchal, 1981).

Ψ Research evidence for internals showing less obedience in a Milgram situation (Holland, 1967).

Ψ Externals more readily give themselves electric shocks (Miller, 1975)!

Ψ Independent behaviour and internal locus of control are linked to high self-esteem (Sterbin & Rakow, 1996).

Ψ Independent behaviour and internal locus of control are linked to low authoritarianism (De Man et al., 1993).

Evaluation

Ψ The attribution theory can account for individual differences in conformity and obedience.

Ψ What does locus of control correlate with and why should this be the case?

Ψ The general nature of the locus of control scale may not generalise well to specific situations.

Ψ Psychopaths would obey in a Milgram situation because of internal factors, which is the opposite of what attribution theory predicts!

Ψ It is oversimplified: individuals are unlikely to be solely internal or external and there are other internal and external factors than just locus of control. Give examples of these.

Ψ Internal and external factors are not separate from each other.

Implications of Research into Conformity, Obedience, and Independence for Social Change

For details see Eysenck's textbook (pages 303–308) and Brody and Dwyer's revision guide (pages 160–162). Fill in the gaps using the letter clues provided and use the cues in the table to guide your note taking.

The i_____ of the s_____ i_____ research initially appear disturbing because Milgram's research suggests we are capable of great inhumanity in the name of o_____ and Asch's research shows the strength of the pressures to c_____ given that this occurred in a quite ridiculous situation. This suggests we are all capable of b_____ obedience and m_____ss conformity in the right situation! This suggests that e_____ behaviour lies within all of us.

Implications of research into conformity

Ψ Negative implications: the higher conformity to friends is of great concern.

Ψ Positive implications:
  - The situation in the study rarely occurs in real life.

  - The majority showed independence rather than conformity.

  - Time and context may have decreased conformity.

Implications of research into obedience

Ψ Negative implications:
  - The blind obedience and blame placed on the victim as a consequence shows great inhumanity.

  - It has been argued that Milgram's research is so artificial it has few implications for real life, but Hofling et al.'s (1966) research with nurses and the Strip Search Prank Call Scam (Wolfson, 2005) suggest otherwise.

  - Nazi Germany, Rwanda genocide, and torture of prisoners at Abu Ghraib prison in Iraq show the all too real consequences of blind obedience.

Ψ Positive implications:
  - The implications of Milgram's research are limited because the situation is very artificial and so the obedience shown in Milgram's research is not the same as the 'obedience' shown in the real-life atrocities such as Nazi Germany.

  - Social support is a powerful limiting factor on obedience and this is usually present in real-life situations.

Implications of research into independent behaviour

Ψ Negative implications: Millions of people have an external locus of control, a lack of self-esteem, or are high in authoritarianism, or all three.

Ψ Positive implications: Individuals with an internal locus of control, high in self-esteem, and low in authoritarianism are capable of independent behaviour.

Promoting social change

Ψ Provide social support (Milgram, 1974, and Asch, 1956).

Ψ Give time to reflect on moral behaviour (Sherman, 1980).

Ψ Encourage individualism and personal responsibility (Kashima & Kashima, 2003).

Ψ Nurture self-esteem (Arndt et al., 2002).

Ψ Reduce hierarchical structures.

Ψ Educate—the actual participants in Milgram and Asch's research provide strong support for this.

Conclusions

The focus of this section on social change has been for the need to d_____ obedience and conformity. This is not always desirable as there are many occasions where it is optimal to o_____ or c_____. So don't come to the conclusion that all forms of s_____ i_____ should be avoided. Our desire to fit in and so c_____ has important personal and social benefits in terms of a sense of belonging and the s_____ cohesion of society; and of course it is rarely appropriate to d_____ your teacher or your boss! So whilst we should avoid blind obedience and mindless conformity, these influences in themselves are not n_____. To decide which is the appropriate response, c_____, o_____, or i_____, think about the consequences of the behaviour!

Using this in the exam: Social influence in everyday life

You may be asked:

Short answer AO1 questions

1. Outline explanations of independent behaviour.
2. Outline individual differences in independent behaviour.

Short answer AO2 questions

1. Explain factors that increase resistance to obedience.
2. Explain factors that increase resistance to conformity.
3. Explain the effect of the locus of control on independent behaviour.

Short answer AO3 questions

1. Assess the validity of research into resistance.
2. Assess the validity of research into individual differences in independent behaviour.
3. Discuss one methodological issue of research into….resistance, individual differences…

Long answer questions

These can be either 8 marks or 12 marks, where AO1: AO2 is 50 : 50 so be prepared to give a shorter or longer version of this answer depending on whether the question is 8 or 12 marks.

1. Discuss research into the influence that individual differences have on independent behaviour. (8 or 12 marks)

Paragraph 1 AO1 Outline the locus of control as an individual difference.

Milgram was sceptical about the importance of individual differences in terms of the results of his study. However, describe how Modigliani and Rochat (1995) have shown the effect of individual differences in Milgram's study. Explain the locus of control: attribution theory (Rotter, 1966), and how this would affect susceptibility to the agentic state in Milgram's study; and susceptibility to normative influence in Asch's study.

Paragraph 2 AO2 Evaluate the research into the locus of control.

Assess how far you think the locus of control is a key determinant of independent behaviour. Some studies have found no relationship between locus of control and majority influence (Williams & Warchal, 1981). However, another has found a clear effect of locus of control on obedience in a study that involved participants giving themselves electric shocks (Miller, 1975)! Discuss the fact that there is not a clear link between locus of control and independent behaviour as self-esteem is another key variable. The fact that these locus of control and self-esteem correlate is predictable and strengthens the argument that locus of control is a key determinant of independent behaviour. Furthermore, because locus of control cannot be manipulated, cause and effect cannot be inferred. Further weaknesses include the fact that the locus of control is too general a measure and so cannot predict with accuracy how individuals will behave in Milgram and Asch scenarios, not least because there are multiple internal and external factors in these scenarios and so it is too simplistic to say internals will be independent and externals will obey or conform because they will be more influenced by the situational (external) factors. The fact that the majority did conform in Asch's study at least once, and the majority obeyed in Milgram's study, can be used as evidence that situational factors override individual factors when the situational pressures are great.

2. Critically consider the implications for social change of research into social influence.

(8 or 12 marks)

Paragraph 1 AO1 Outline implications of social influence research.

Explain why the implications of social influence research appear initially quite negative! For example, they suggest that the majority of us are capable of evil and mindless behaviour—why? Use later studies by Hofling et al. (1966) and the Strip Search Prank Call Scam (Wolfson, 2005) to show the worrying consequence of blind obedience.

Paragraph 2 AO2 Discuss the implications.

Challenge the validity of the implications you have just described. The conformity shown in Asch's study may not be valid due to the artificiality of the research; the fact there was no time for discussion, and it can even be argued that Asch's study has positive implications because it is more an example of independent behaviour—why? Milgram's research can also be challenged in terms of the artificiality and the lack of social support, which mean that such blind obedience is less likely in real life. The temporal validity of the studies can be questioned as this also limits negative implications. However, to protect society against blind obedience and mindless conformity, a number of key implications that have emerged are: the need for social support; provide people with time to think about their actions; reduce the status differences in hierarchical organisations; education and learning—explain how these are key ways to defuse social influence. Discuss the fact that it is not always desirable to show resistance because society needs obedience and conformity!

Psychopathology Learning Objectives

On completion of this topic you should be familiar with the following.

Defining and explaining psychological abnormality

- Outline and evaluate the definitions that are used to establish whether someone is abnormal: statistical infrequency, deviation from social norms, deviation from ideal mental health, and failure to function adequately.
- Critically consider the issue of cultural relativism in terms of the definitions of abnormality.
- Outline the key assumptions made on the causes of abnormality by the models of abnormality, i.e., explain what the causes of abnormality are according to the biological and psychological (psychodynamic, behavioural, and cognitive) models of abnormality.
- Evaluate the biological and psychological (including behavioural, psychodynamic, and cognitive) models of abnormality.

Treating abnormality

- Outline and evaluate biological therapies, including drugs and ECT.
- Outline and evaluate psychological therapies, including psychoanalysis, systematic desensitisation, and Cognitive Behavioural Therapy.

Cross-reference the above learning objectives with the Specification and fill in the self-assessment box below on completion of the topic.

SELF-ASSESSMENT BOX

☺ **Which of the above do you know?**

☹ **Are there any gaps in your knowledge that need to be targeted during revision?**

Defining Psychological Abnormality

For details, see Eysenck's textbook (pages 275–284) and Brody and Dwyer's revision guide (pages 169–171). Use the cues in the table to guide your note taking and fill in the gaps using the letter clues provided.

Definition of abnormality

Deviation from social norms

Description

Behaviour that deviates from the n_____ and v_____ of society, that is, the approved and expected ways of b_____g in a particular society, is considered to be abnormal. According to the social norms definition, behaviour is abnormal when it is undesirable for society and so is classed as socially d _____t behaviour.

Ψ Give examples of behaviour that deviates from social norms:

Evaluation

Ψ Subjectivity and era-dependence of moral codes.

Ψ Culturally relative.

Ideal mental health

Description

This is based on the h_____ approach and so the emphasis is on fulfilling one's potential, which is called s_____-a_____. Jahoda (1958) suggested six 'elements for optimal living':

1. S_____-a_____
2. P_____ g_____
3. I_____
4. A_____
5. P_____ of r_____
6. E_____ m_____

Evaluation

Ψ The focus on positive characteristics is good.

Ψ Culturally relative, as not all of the characteristics generalise to collectivist cultures, e.g., autonomy.

Ψ The criteria for ideal mental health are vague and idealistic. Many people would fail to achieve ideal mental health.

Failure to function adequately

Description

Failure to function adequately refers to failure to fulfil in_____, s_____, and o_____ roles. Rosenhan and Seligman (1989) suggested seven features of abnormality:

1. S_____
2. M_____
3. V_____ and u_____ of behaviour
4. U_____ and l_____ of c_____
5. I_____ and i_____
6. O_____ d_____
7. V_____ of m_____ and i_____ s_____

Evaluation

Ψ Value judgements mean assessment is difficult and may be unreliable.

Ψ Culturally relative, as judgements will be influenced by cultural norms, e.g., unconventionality.

Ψ Not all people have self-insight into their failure to function.

The multi-perspective approach to defining abnormality

The difficulty in defining abnormality has led to the conclusion that there is no precise distinction between abnormal and normal, and so a continuum is the best way to define abnormality. This is normally distributed with normal and abnormal at either end and most people fall somewhere in the middle.

NORMAL *(Where do you fall on the continuum?)* ABNORMAL

←─────────────────────────────────────→

The key criticism of *all* definitions of abnormality is cultural relativism.

So what is cultural relativism?

Explain why cultural relativism is a key weakness of the definitions of abnormality.

Conclusions

None of the d_____ offers a universal means of identifying a_____The f_____ to f_____n may have more real-world validity as the global assessment of functioning, which is used as part of the diagnosis of mental disorder using DSM is based on social, occupational, and psychological functioning. Thus, ability to f_____n is perhaps the most v_____d way to assess abnormality/normality as it is more focused in reality than the idealistic ideal mental health. Two of the most common indicators of abnormality are personal s_____g and d_____r (harm) to others, both of which are features of the failure to function definition and are UNIVERSAL signs of abnormality. Thus, the definition has been usefully applied to real life, and has some degree of u_____y, but caution must be taken as ethnocentrism and value j_____s can bias the defining of abnormality using this definition.

Find out for yourself: To enhance your use of cultural relativism as an evaluation point, complete an internet search of culture-bound syndromes such as koro, amok, and brain fag.

Models of Abnormality

For details, see Eysenck's textbook (pages 284–299) and Brody and Dwyer's revision guide (pages 171–178). Fill in the gaps using the letter clues provided and use the cues in the table to guide your note taking.

Biological (medical) model	
Description This model uses p_____l i_____s as a model for psychological disorder. Thus, abnormality has physical c_____ such as b_____ dysfunction (neurological), biochemical imbalances, infection, or genetics, and so can only be cured through m_____. It is the dominant model as medical practitioners naturally favour it but it has been expanded upon by the d_____–stress model, which sees abnormality as an interaction of g_____ pre_____ and e_____.	
Assumptions on the causes of abnormality Ψ Infection. Ψ Genetic factors. Ψ Biochemistry. Ψ Neuroanatomy.	**Evaluation** Ψ Research evidence is based on well-established science. Ψ The model has validity as it successfully explains phenylketonuria (PKU). Ψ It does provide insights into schizophrenia and depression. Ψ The analogy to physical illness is limited. Ψ Concordance rates are not 100%. Ψ Cause and effect is not clear. Ψ Does not give enough consideration to psychological and social factors and so is biologically deterministic and reductionist. Ψ Anti-psychiatry, e.g. Szasz's 'problems in living'. Ψ Ethical implications.

Psychodynamic model

Description

This model focuses on the dynamics of the mind. According to F_____, the mind is like an iceberg with the tip representing conscious thought, and the majority representing the preconscious and the u_____, which we are unaware of and cannot access. Material is r_____ into the un_____ if it is a source of c_____t. The unconscious develops during c_____ and is the key motivator of adult thinking and behaviour. Thus, conflicts during childhood that have not been re_____ are the cause of abnormality.

Assumptions on the causes of abnormality

Ψ Conflict between the id, ego, and superego.

Ψ Fixation at psychosexual stages due to conflict.

Ψ Defence mechanisms that help control conflict.

Evaluation

Ψ Positive implications of Freud's work—psychoanalysis paved the way for later psychological models.

Ψ Evidence does support childhood as a factor in the development of abnormality.

Ψ Does not give enough consideration to adult experiences and can be criticised as being deterministic.

Ψ Overemphasis on sexual factors and underemphasis on social factors.

Ψ Clinical interview was the main research method and so there is a lack of scientific evidence.

Ψ Concepts are vague and cannot be operationalised, and so cannot be verified or falsified.

Ψ Ethical implications.

Behavioural model

Description

This model is based on the principles of l_____ and the assumption that all behaviour is learned through a_____ (c_____ conditioning), r_____ (o_____ conditioning), or social learning (s_____ l_____ t_____). Abnormality is a result of learning mal_____ and dysfunctional b_____.

Assumptions on the causes of abnormality

Ψ Classical conditioning (Pavlov, 1927).

Ψ Operant conditioning (Skinner, 1938).

Ψ Social learning theory (Bandura, 1965).

Evaluation

Ψ Operant conditioning and observational learning account for much human learning and so have validity as explanations of abnormality.

Ψ Difficult to evidence the real-life conditioning history of people with abnormality.

Ψ Underlying causes are ignored because the behaviourists refuse to investigate internal processes. They investigate only that which is observable and measurable, i.e., behaviour, and so ignore the influence of cognition and emotion.

Ψ Consequently therapies treat symptoms not causes.

Ψ The behavioural therapies do work well for phobias.

Ψ Exaggerates the importance of environmental factors and so is environmentally deterministic.

Ψ Extrapolation of Pavlov's and Skinner's research from animals must be questioned.

Ψ Artificiality of lab research means ecological validity can be questioned.

Ψ Oversimplified and so reductionist.

Ψ Ethical implications.

Cognitive model

Description

This model suggests cognitive d_____ underpins abnormality. The individual is an inf_____ pro_____ and it is a breakdown in c_____ processing that causes abnormality. Irrational, obsessive, and faulty thinking can affect e_____ and b_____.

Assumptions on the causes of abnormality

Ψ Distorted cognition/faulty thinking/ irrational thoughts. Which common irrational thoughts do Newmark et al. (1973) provide examples of?

Ψ Beck's (1976) cognitive triad.

Ψ Lewinsohn et al.'s (2001) research on faulty thinking and depression.

Ψ A breakdown in information processing— the computer analogy.

Evaluation

Ψ The model has validity (i.e., truth) as it helps to explain anxiety disorders and depression.

Ψ Cause and effect is not clear.

Ψ The cognitive model has led to the development of Cognitive Behavioural Therapy, which has proved to be highly effective.

Ψ The cognitive model is not explanatory— what does it not explain?

Ψ May lack relevance to disorders other than depression and anxiety.

Ψ Ignores other important factors such as genetics and social factors.

Ψ Ethical implications.

Conclusion: The multi-dimensional approach

To fully understand ab_____ b_____ a multi-dimensional approach is necessary that draws from all of the m_____ of a_____. A particularly useful example is expressed by the diathesis–stress model that takes into account the interaction of g_____ pre_____ (diathesis) and en_____ (stress) to explain psychological disorder. Thus, according to the d_____–s_____ model, 'the g____ loads the gun but the e_____t pulls the trigger'.

Find out for yourself: Imagine someone has just described their feelings of depression to you and lacks any understanding of why they feel like this. How would you summarise the models of abnormality to explain their condition? Which explanations do you think have most validity?

Using this in the exam:
Defining and explaining abnormality

You may be asked:

Short answer AO1 questions

1. Recognise descriptions of the definitions of abnormality.
2. Outline any one (which would be specified) of the definitions of abnormality.
3. Outline key features of any one (which would be specified) of the models of abnormality/psychopathology.

Short answer AO2 questions

1. Explain how any one (which would be specified) of the models of abnormality would account for the mental state of an individual described in the stimulus.
2. Give a limitation of any one (which would be specified) of the definitions of abnormality.
3. Explain how the biological model differs from the…(any one of the other models) in the way it explains abnormality.

Short answer AO3 questions

1. Explain one way in which the biological, psychodynamic, behavioural, cognitive model has been investigated in research.
2. Give one criticism of the validity of research into any one of the models of abnormality.
3. Explain the ethical issues of any one of the models of abnormality.

Long answer questions

These can be either 8 marks or 12 marks, where AO1:AO2 is 50:50 so be prepared to give a shorter or longer version of this answer depending on whether the question is 8 or 12 marks.

1. Outline and evaluate the deviation from social norms definition of abnormality. (8 or 12 marks)

Paragraph 1 AO1 Outline the key features of the definition.

Outline the deviation from social norms definition using examples to illustrate your answer, such as homosexuality.

Paragraph 2 AO2 Evaluate the lack of cultural relativism of the definition using cross-cultural differences to support this evaluation.

The social norms definition of abnormality is culturally biased as it is based on individualistic culture. Cross-cultural differences in conceptions of abnormality are evidence for wide cultural variations, e.g., sexuality (an example being the Dani society of New Guinea who wait two years after marriage before having sex and after the birth of the child there is a period of abstinence for 4–6 years), drugs (cannabis is used to access the spirit world in some cultures and is a recreational drug in others), and social customs (in the Inuit culture having hallucinations and visions confers Shaman status as it's thought to mean one is in contact with the spirits). These show that normal/abnormal are social constructions and so change across time periods and cultures. Also cross-cultural differences in diagnosis (women are 40% more likely than men to be admitted to mental hospitals; Afro-Caribbeans are 2–7 times more likely to be diagnosed with schizophrenia than are white patients), and the existence of culture-bound syndromes (koro and windigo are good examples) all support the fact that abnormality is defined differently across cultures. The fact that there is a long history of abnormality being used as a way of controlling dissidents (Russia; China; labelled as insane if disagreed with government; witch hunts were also a form of social control) shows that what is and isn't abnormal differs across cultures. Szasz (1989) claims the main function of the label 'abnormal' is social control; it is given to those who do not conform to social norms and of course these change across cultures.

2. Outline and evaluate the failure to function adequately definition of abnormality.   (8 or 12 marks)

Paragraph 1 AO1 Outline the key features of the definition.

Outline the seven abnormal characteristics that determine failure to function. Explain that this allows degree of functioning to be assessed based on the ability to fulfil social, occupational, and personal roles.

Paragraph 2 AO2 Assess the lack of cultural relativism of the definition, consider the issue of value judgements and the real-world validity of the definition.

Assess the cultural relativity of interpretations of behaviour, i.e., what would be considered bizarre, irrational, environmental mastery, incomprehensible, violation of moral and ideal standards depends on culturally constructed norms. USE EXAMPLES TO SUPPORT THIS, such as sexuality, attitudes to drugs, social customs and rituals (wodaabe beauty contest for selecting husbands). Conclude that the definitions are Western biased as they are based on Western ideals. You could use research on diagnosis such as Cooper who found African-Americans were seven times more likely to be diagnosed with schizophrenia than white Americans and link this to the ethnocentrism inherent in interpreting the behaviour of other cultures. Consider that the definition involves VALUE JUDGEMENTS and so assessments of abnormality would be ethnocentric and culture-biased. This means the reliability (consistency) and validity (truth) of judgements about abnormality are issues. Era-dependence is also an issue—explain why using an example such as the fact that homosexuality was classed as a failure to function in previous time periods. A global assessment of functioning is used as part of the DSM criteria in the diagnosis of mental disorders—consider how this shows the real-world usefulness of the definition.

3. Discuss the ideal mental health definition of abnormality.   (8 or 12 marks)

Paragraph 1 AO1 Outline the key features of the definition.

Outline the deviation from ideal mental health by identifying Jahoda's six elements for optimal living. Explain that it is when some of these elements are absent and so the individual is blocked from achieving self-actualisation that abnormality develops. Explain what self-actualisation is and how this is based on the humanistic perspective.

Paragraph 2 AO2 Assess the lack of cultural relativism and the issue of value judgements, and evaluate the positive approach taken by the definition as both a strength and a weakness.

Assess the cultural relativity of autonomy as it is an individualistic not collectivistic ideal. Also assess the cultural relativity of interpretations of behaviour, i.e., what would be considered environmental mastery depends on culturally-constructed norms. USE EXAMPLES TO SUPPORT THIS, such as sexuality, attitudes to drugs, social customs and rituals (wodaabe beauty contest for selecting husbands). Conclude the definitions are Western biased as they are based on Western ideals. You could use research on diagnosis such as Cooper who found that African-Americans were seven times more likely to be diagnosed with schizophrenia that white Americans and link this to culture-bias and ethnocentrism in interpreting the behaviour of other cultures. The ideal mental health definition involves VALUE JUDGEMENTS and so assessments of abnormality would be ethnocentric and culture-biased. This means reliability (consistency) and validity (truth) of judgements about abnormality are issues. Era-dependence is also an issue because social constructions can change over time—elaborate. You could also discuss the fact that the ideal mental health definition takes a more positive approach to abnormality compared to other definitions. This can be seen as a positive and a negative—explain that the elements are too challenging, we cannot all realise these; this does not make us all abnormal! It has been suggested that self-actualisation is more accessible to the upper and middle classes and so the population validity of ideal mental health can be questioned. Explain how this limits validity.

4. Critically consider the biological model of psychopathology.   (8 or 12 marks)

Paragraph 1 AO1 Outline the key features of the model.

Outline the biological model, e.g., that it assumes mental illness is similar to physical illness; it is the dominant model of abnormality and proposes that abnormality has physical causes such as genetics, biochemicals, and neuroanatomy. Elaborate—for example, outline the biochemical explanation of schizophrenia; the genetic and neuroanatomy explanations of eating disorders.

Paragraph 2 AO2 Discuss strengths and weaknesses.

Strengths include the fact it is based on well-established science and the focus on a physical cause means that the patient is not blamed for their illness. However, on the other hand, the fact that responsibility is taken away from the individual does raise ethical implications. However, weaknesses include a lack of evidence such as that there are no 100% concordance rates in genetic studies so genetics cannot be the only factor. Cause and effect is an issue with biochemical and neuroanatomy explanations. Also anti-psychiatrists such as Szasz argue that we should take into account 'sick society' rather than focusing on the 'sick individual'. Anti-psychiatrists claim that abnormality is NOT due to biology, that the biological model just offers a form of 'social control' over those who deviate from the norms of society. The model is biologically deterministic and reductionist—WHY? Most importantly it ignores nurture and psychological causes of abnormality, e.g., internal factors as covered by the psychodynamic (psyche and unconscious conflicts) and cognitive (faulty thinking), and external factors (the environment) as covered by the behavioural model. Do not just describe the alternative models of abnormality, use them as counter-perspectives. To achieve, explain what they offer to our understanding of abnormality that the biological model does not. Consider that no single model accounts for abnormality; it exists at a number of levels and so the diathesis–stress model may offer us a better understanding—explain.

5. Outline and evaluate the psychodynamic model of abnormality.   (8 or 12 marks)

Paragraph 1 AO1 Outline the key features of the model.

Outline the psychodynamic model, e.g., Freud introduced psychology to abnormality and emphasised the internal dynamics of the mind, and suggest abnormality is caused by unconscious conflicts that lead to fixation and regression (elaborate). Treatment is psychoanalysis, 'the talking cure', and this involves free association and dream analysis, 'the royal road to the unconscious' (elaborate).

Paragraph 2 AO2 Discuss strengths and weaknesses.

Evaluate: Strengths include introducing psychological cause to mental illness; childhood does play a part; the competing desires of the id, ego, and superego has face validity—WHY? However, not enough attention is paid to later adult experience and there is an overemphasis on sexual factors and underemphasis on social factors. Methodological weaknesses are: researcher bias of the clinical interview, including selectivity in the examples Freud drew from the case studies, and ignoring alternative explanations and information that didn't support his theories. He never took notes during the therapy session—consider how this may have led to selectivity. Sample bias—middle-class, hysterical Viennese women are not representative of other populations or other types of abnormality. Most importantly, Freud's concepts cannot be tested very easily because they are vague and cannot be measured (e.g., how do we measure penis envy?). What does this mean? Clue: verification and falsification are issues and so his theory lacks scientific validity. Freud's theories are also deterministic (because he says behaviour is controlled by biological desires and early childhood experience, which ignores the individual's ability to control his or her own behaviour) and reductionist (too oversimplified).

6. Discuss the behavioural model of abnormality.   (8 or 12 marks)

Paragraph 1 AO1 Outline the key features of the model.

Explain how the abnormality may be learned from the environment through either classical conditioning, operant conditioning, or social learning theory (Bandura, 1965). Use mental disorders such as phobias, depression, and eating disorders to illustrate the learning processes.

Paragraph 2 AO2 Discuss strengths and weaknesses.

Consider the strengths of the model, for example behavioural therapies are particularly effective for phobias and a further strength is that it tends to be non-judgemental of the individual as it is assumed that abnormality is learned from the environment and so the individual is not responsible. However, limitations include the fact that underlying causes are ignored because the behaviourists refuse to investigate internal processes. They investigate only that which is observable and measurable—explain what underlying causes are ignored by the model. Consequently, therapies may treat symptoms not causes, and so symptom substitution may occur, which is when another disorder develops because the causes of the initial disorder have not been treated. The behavioural model exaggerates the importance of environmental factors and so is environmentally deterministic—explain what this means. Extrapolation of Pavlov's and Skinner's research from animals can also be questioned. Research into conditioning is artificial and this means external validity can be questioned. For example, the Little Albert case study has been difficult to replicate. The ethical implications of the therapies also raise concern—why? Consider the reductionism of the model and why the diathesis–stress model may offer a more comprehensive understanding.

7. Outline and evaluate the cognitive model of psychopathology. (8 or 12 marks)

Paragraph 1 AO1 Outline the key features of the model.

Explain how a breakdown in cognitive processing explains abnormality according to the cognitive model. Consider two key assumptions of this model 1) the 'computer analogy' and 2) the faulty thinking that results from a breakdown in processing. Use examples to illustrate faulty thinking such as Beck's cognitive triad where the individual has maladaptive thoughts about the self, world, and future; and cognitive biases suggested by Beck such as magnification and 'all or nothing' thinking. Explain that faulty thinking can affect emotions and behaviour and that the cause of the abnormality is rooted within the individual; it is their thought processes causing the abnormality.

Paragraph 2 AO2 Discuss strengths and weaknesses.

The model has validity (i.e., truth) as there is no doubt that distorted and irrational thinking does characterise mental disorders. However, it may be relevant to anxiety and depression more than other mental disorders. Also, cause and effect is not clear—why not? Key strengths of the model include the fact that the cognitive-behavioural model has developed from it and has proven even more effective at treating mental disorders than either model on its own—explain. A further strength is the responsibility is placed on the patient and this can empower patients to take control of their mental well-being. However, individual responsibility also raises negative ethical implications—why? The model is also criticised as being descriptive, not explanatory. A further weakness is that it ignores other important factors such as genetics and social factors: Machine reductionism is an issue—why? Use the diathesis–stress model to explain why the cognitive model only provides a partial understanding of abnormality.

Treatments of Abnormality

For details, see Eysenck's textbook (pages 303–324) and Brody and Dwyer's revision guide (pages 178–186). Fill in the gaps using the letter clues provided and use the cues in the table to guide your note taking.

Biological therapies

Description

According to the biological model abnormality has physical c_____ and so can only be cured through m_____ treatments, which involve manipulation of the b_____.

Drug therapy

Ψ Anti-depressant drugs—what do they act upon?
- MAOIs

- Tricyclics

- Selective serotonin re-uptake inhibitors (SSRIs).

- Lithium as a treatment for bipolar disorder.

Ψ Anti-anxiety drugs—what do they act upon?
- Benzodiazepines

- Buspirone

Ψ Anti-psychotics—what do they act upon?
- Neuroleptic drugs

- Atypical drugs

Electroconvulsive therapy (ECT)

Ψ What does this involve?

Ψ When is ECT used?

Evaluation of ECT

Ψ How effective is ECT in the treatment of depression and schizophrenia?

Ψ Lack understanding of how it works.

Ψ Side effects.

Ψ Less effective for some patients with depression.

Ψ No clear long-term benefits for patients with schizophrenia.

Overall evaluation of drug therapy

Ψ Effectiveness.

Ψ Relapse rate.

Ψ Lack understanding of why drugs work.

Ψ Drug dependence.

Ψ Drop-out rate.

Ψ Side effects.

Ψ Placebo effect.

Cognitive Behavioural Therapy (CBT)

Description

This therapy combines c_____ and b_____ therapy and so treats mental illness with a combined approach where both maladaptive b_____ and dysfunctional t_____ are treated. Challenging patients to t_____ about themselves and the world, in particular their i_____ bias (a tendency to interpret ambiguous situations in a n_____ way), and changing their b_____ are the key goals of therapy.

Ψ Beck's (1976) CBT: How is this both cognitive and behavioural?

Ψ How effective is CBT (Butler et al., 2006)?

Ψ The use of video feedback (Harvey et al., 2000).

Ψ Treating behaviour by not using safety-seeking behaviours.

Evaluation

Ψ The combination of approaches is more effective.

Ψ Sound research basis.

Ψ Effective across a range of disorders.

Ψ Less effective than family intervention in the treatment of schizophrenia.

Ψ The effects of changing faulty cognitions may be exaggerated.

Ψ Cognitions may be realistic to patients' difficult lives!

Ψ Ignores other influential factors, e.g., b_____ and c_____ experiences.

Ψ The combined approach means it is difficult to know which components have most effect.

Ψ May treat symptoms not causes—why?

Conclusions

Any comparisons of the effectiveness of different t_____ should be treated with caution as it is difficult to know if differences are due to the actual therapy or the individual differences of the p_____ or t_____. Moreover, recovery may not be due to the specific nature of the treatment but due to general factors that underpin all treatments, such as having someone s_____ to talk to and being able to express all w_____ and fe_____. Assessing the effectiveness of treatments is further complicated by the 'hello-goodbye effect' whereby patients overestimate their s_____ at the start of t_____ and underestimate their symptoms at the end. Another issue is publication b_____ whereby significant findings are published more than non-significant ones. Both of these biases may make therapies appear more e_____ than they really are! The power to suppress research findings is another concern often levelled at dr_____ companies where findings have suggested the product is d_____!

Using this in the exam: Treating abnormality

You may be asked:

Short answer AO1 questions

1. Outline the key features of drug therapy/ECT/psychoanalysis/systematic desensitisation/cognitive behavioural therapy.

Short answer AO2 questions

1. Explain how… (one of the therapies would be specified) might be carried out.

Short answer AO3 questions

1. Explain one ethical issue with ECT/psychoanalysis/systematic desensitisation/cognitive behavioural therapy.
2. Explain one methodological issue with assessing the effectiveness of the therapies.

Long answer questions

These can be either 8 marks or 12 marks, where AO1: AO2 is 50 : 50 so be prepared to give a shorter or longer version of this answer depending on whether the question is 8 or 12 marks.

1. Discuss the effectiveness of biological therapies.   (8 or 12 marks)

Paragraph 1 AO1/2 Outline and evaluate anti-depressants.
Identify the main types of drug therapy such as anti-depressants, anti-anxiety drugs, and anti-psychotics. Explain the biological mechanisms by which anti-depressants such as MAOIs, tricyclics, and SSRIs work. Then compare the effectiveness of the different types of anti-depressants.

Paragraph 2 AO1/AO2 Outline and evaluate anti-anxiety drugs.
Outline the biological mechanism of benzodiazepines and buspirone and compare the effectiveness of the two types of anti-anxiety drugs. Consider the issues of drug therapies in general, such as issues of dependence, tolerance, and side-effects, and whether the drugs treat symptoms and not causes. Relapse is more common after drug therapy than after other types of therapy and drop-out rate is high due to people's aversion to drugs. However, the success of drugs must be recognised—they do help many people cope with very disabling mental illnesses. They have been evaluated as having the same or very similar effectiveness to Cognitive Behavioural Therapy (Mitte, 2005, and Barlow et al., 2000), which is evidence of success. However, drugs do not work for all patients and we lack understanding as to why they work for some and not others, as we lack insight into *how* the drugs work.

2. Outline and evaluate psychoanalysis.   (8 or 12 marks)

Paragraph 1 AO1 Outline the key features of the treatment.
Explain that psychoanalysis is based on accessing repressed memories and explain how this can be achieved through hypnosis, free association, and the analysis of dreams. Explain the role of transference in therapy and use the case studies such as that of Anna O to illustrate the therapy.

Paragraph 2 AO2 Consider strengths and weaknesses of the treatment.

Provide evidence for the role of childhood in abnormality and so evidence for the validity of accessing repressed memories from childhood as a treatment (Kendler et al., 1996). However, also consider evidence against as recent events are ignored (Kendler et al., 1998). False memory syndrome is a concern; it is impossible to test how much insight contributes to recovery and transference does not seem to have the positive effects Freud attributed to it. Matt and Navarro (1997) completed a thorough consideration of 63 meta-analyses that compared the effectiveness of different types of therapy. Psychodynamic was 75% more effective than no treatment at all—some would say this is a futile comparison! However, it often compared unfavourably to other types of treatment. Matt and Navarro concluded this may be more linked to the severity of the mental conditions being treated, as those using psychoanalysis tend to have more serious conditions.

3. Critically consider the effectiveness of systematic desensitisation. (8 or 12 marks)

Paragraph 1 AO1 Outline the key features of the treatment.

Explain how systematic desensitisation (SD) developed by Wolpe (1958, 1969) employs the principles of classical conditioning to treat phobias. Outline the stages: muscle relaxation, construct fear hierarchy, face feared objects— beginning by just imagining them and progressing to real-life exposure in many cases. Describe how Wolpe explained the technique worked through reciprocal inhibition. However, it may also work due to extinction—explain.

Paragraph 2 AO2 Consider strengths and weaknesses of the treatment.

It can be evaluated as a successful treatment of phobias, Denholtz, Hall, and Mann (1978) evaluated it as effective in the treatment of flying phobia, although others have concluded it is only moderately effective— why? Discuss how it is not clear which is more effective—reciprocal inhibition or extinction; it may well be the case that reciprocal inhibition is only effective when there is insufficient time for extinction to take place. However, the use of relaxation certainly makes SD a more human treatment than exposure therapy—why? Discuss the limitations of the therapy: it only works for phobias, and has no relevance to other forms of disorder. It can be argued that the phobias treated by it are not as serious as more severe mental conditions; exposure therapy tends to be more effective than SD.

4. Assess the effectiveness of Cognitive Behavioural Therapy. (8 or 12 marks)

Paragraph 1 AO1 Outline the key features of the treatment.

Explain the key principles of Cognitive Behavioural Therapy (CBT) and use specific forms such as Beck's to illustrate how these work in practice. Use the case study given by Clark (1996) of a 40-year-old man with panic disorder to illustrate how the therapy works. Explain how video feedback is used to challenge interpretive biases and how challenging patients' safety-seeking behaviours can reduce phobias.

Paragraph 2 AO2 Consider strengths and weaknesses of the treatment.

Use Butler's (2006) comprehensive review of 16 meta-analyses to argue for the effectiveness of CBT. The combined approach of CBT is what makes it more effective than either form of therapy on its own. However, this does mean we lack understanding of which aspects of it are most effective. It is less effective in the treatment of schizophrenia and other psychotic disorders—why? More adaptive cognitions do not always produce more adaptive behaviour and so perhaps the importance of cognition has been exaggerated. Some cognitions may not be faulty but may instead reflect the difficulties of the individual's life and so there may be too much emphasis on the individual's cognition being 'wrong'. Perhaps the focus is too narrow and so we need to consider social and cultural factors, not just the individual.

Appendix: How to Impress the Examiner on AO2 and AO3

The methodological criticisms in the table below are a useful source of either AO2 or AO3 marks. AO2 because they can be used to provide criticisms in short answer or essay questions, and AO3 because they enable you to evaluate the methodology, results, and impact of experimental research, which the AO3 skill requires you to do.

Examples have been given to show how the criticisms can be related to different topic areas. Fill in some of your own examples in the spaces provided. Positive and negative criticisms have been suggested—note the expression on the face!

Know the jargon and use it!

EXPERIMENTAL

☺ Variables are controlled and so have high internal validity and can infer cause and effect. Can easily replicate to verify reliability, e.g., behaviourism/learning theory (the scientific perspective!).

☹ Artificiality—may elicit the demand characteristics that can threaten internal validity, e.g., Loftus' (1974) research.

☹ External validity—may not generalise well to other settings, e.g., from the laboratory environment to real-life settings. Research lacks mundane realism, e.g., Milgram's (1963, 1974) research.

Other examples include:

Compare with field and quasi-experiments.

CORRELATIONAL

☺ Enables us to see association of variables that cannot be manipulated as an IV, e.g., divorce, and the effect of this on development.

☹ Causation cannot be inferred, as an IV has not been manipulated, e.g., stress and illness.

☹ Other factors/variables may be involved in the relationship, e.g., individual differences in the relationship between stress and illness.

Other examples include:

SELF-REPORT (Questionnaires and interviews)

☺ Economical and practical, a high response can easily be obtained.

☹ Interviewer bias—the formation of questions, implementation (carrying out the research), analysis, and interpretation can all threaten the validity (truth) of the research.

☹ Social desirability bias—people's answers may be distorted because they want to present themselves favourably.

☹ Only information that people are consciously aware of can be extracted; people are often unaware of why they behave in a certain way.

Other examples include:

OBSERVATION

☺ Can gain in-depth data of natural behaviour, which therefore has high validity.

☹ Ethics—if the observation is covert (the participants are not aware they are being watched).

☹ Participant reactivity (the Hawthorne effect)—participants' behaviour may change if they know they are being watched.

Other examples include:

CASE STUDY

☺ In-depth data that consequently has high internal validity as it tends to be meaningful and truthful.

☹ Based on clinical interviews that may be biased, and so internal validity may be questionable.

☹ Limited external validity (population validity) as the findings obtained from one individual are unlikely to be the same for another. Thus, there is low generalisability (external validity), e.g., privation cases such as Genie.

Other examples include:

SAMPLE SIZE

☹ Sample bias—samples that are small, self-selected, or selected on the basis of availability (opportunity sampling), ethnocentric (centred around a specific ethnic type, e.g., a sample involving only Western, white, middle-class Americans is culturally biased), androcentric (male-centred), or only involve a restricted population, all lack generalisability because they are not very representative and so are biased samples. The results would have low population validity, as generalisability to other populations would be limited. For example, the social influence studies of Milgram (1963, 1974) and Asch (1952) were self-selected, ethnocentric, and androcentric.

Other examples include:

CONFOUNDING VARIABLES

☹ Participant variables—e.g., individual differences in stress and attachments.

☹ Situational variables—factors in the environment affecting the results, e.g., distraction, noise, temperature, time of day.

Other examples include:

Confounding variables threaten internal validity, as in an experiment the IV may not be responsible for the effect on the DV if confounding variables are not controlled. In a correlation, other factors besides the two variables being investigated may be involved in the association.

VALIDITY

Internal validity—the validity of the research within the research context. If research is valid it is likely to be reliable.

☺ If research has internal validity then it is assumed that it has truth. The effect or relationship on the DV, which is caused by the IV, is psychologically real. Therefore, the research measured what it set out to rather than some other factor such as bias or confounding variables.

Other examples include:

External validity—the validity of the research outside the research context.

☹ Ecological validity—lacks generalisability to other settings, e.g., Loftus (1974).

☹ Population validity—lacks generalisability to other populations, e.g., if it uses WWMCA as 90+% of all research does (Western, white middle-class, American sample; remember as modified YMCA).

☹ Temporal validity—lacks generalisability to other time periods as the research may be dated. The date of the research is a possible evaluation point. Contextualise the historical, political, social, and cultural contexts.These can influence the research and so it may lack generalisability to the current context. For example, Bowlby's (1946) research reflected the historical, social, and cultural context, and also the political agenda of the time.

☹ Real-life applications of the research—does the theory or explanation work in real-life? Does it have truth and so does it have value? Does the work add to our understanding? You should assess this on all essay questions.

Other examples include:

RELIABILITY

☺ If research has reliability it has consistency, e.g., the same results are produced over time or by different researchers. Repeating the research is called replication. This is used to establish reliability and validity as replication is usually only possible if the research has internal validity.

☺ Lack of consistency means that validity must also be questioned, e.g., the contradictory psychodynamic explanation of eating disorders. Whereas reliability supports validity as it suggests that the results are psychologically real.

Other examples include:

VALUE FREE vs. VALUE LADEN

☹ Research should not be distorted by researcher bias, it should be free from value judgements (objective not subjective). However, gender, culture, and nature bias all demonstrate value judgements. It can be argued that all research is value laden to some extent.

Other examples include:

DETERMINISM

☹ Biological determinism—the biological approach claims behaviour is determined by the genes, and so ignores the free will of the individual to determine their own behaviour.

☹ Physiological determinism—an explanation that claims physiological processes determine behaviour, and so ignores free will, e.g., hormonal imbalances or brain dysfunction as explanations of abnormality.

☹ Environmental determinism—the behavioural approach claims behaviour is determined by the environment, and so ignores free will, e.g., behaviourism/learning theory.

☹ Psychic determinism—the psychodynamic approach claims adult behaviour is determined by early childhood experience and that behaviour is determined by biological instincts and so ignores free will.

Other examples include:

REDUCTIONISM

☹ Oversimplified explanations that explain a complex phenomenon in terms of only one component. Biological (evolutionary), physiological, and environmental are all forms of reductionism and the above examples for determinism apply. Research may also be criticised for experimental reductionism, e.g., Asch's (1952) study of majority influence and the memory experiments in the 'Human memory' section of this workbook.

Other examples include:

NATURE/NURTURE

☹ Research often takes one perspective at the expense of the other. For example, biological explanations of eating disorders can be criticised for ignoring nurture and vice versa for the psychological explanations.

☺ A compromise position between nature and nurture is offered by the diathesis–stress model, and this interactionist perspective of the influence of genes and the environment offers a more comprehensive approach to understanding behaviour.

Other examples include:

ETHICS

☺ A cost–benefit analysis should precede all research. This involves deciding 'do the ends justify the means?'

☹ The breaking of ethical guidelines (deception, informed consent, right to withdraw, confidentiality, protection of participants) and socially sensitive research (research that has consequences for vulnerable groups, e.g., gender or culturally biased research) may be considered ethically injustifiable. For example, ethics is the critical issue in the 'Social influence' section so Milgram's (1963, 1974) and Asch's (1952) research can be criticised on ethical grounds.

Other examples include:

Essay questions require much more than a list of evaluation points, so please contextualise the above criticisms. You must fully relate any of the criticisms you use to the question to make sure they are relevant and not just add-ons. The latter, of course, might constitute good evaluation but would receive few marks if it does not answer the question. So assess the consequences of the criticisms by asking yourself: so what does this mean in terms of the question? Thus, make conclusions with respect to the question throughout your answer. For example, if validity is questioned you can conclude that the theory/research/explanation may lack truth and so explanatory power is limited as it does not offer meaningful insights. Elaborating the criticism like this gains more credit than simply identifying strengths and weaknesses.

See the 'Step-by-step guide to answering exam questions' in the 'Basics' section for more information on essay technique.

NOTES

NOTES

Psychoanalysis—the 'talking cure'

Description

This treatment is based on F_____'s theory and so focuses on the dynamics of the mind. It is known as the 't_____ c_____'. The therapies are based on Freud's key assumption that abnormality is due to internal c_____s, which are r_____d, and which lead to r_____, i.e., going back to an earlier s_____ of ps_____ development. The more serious the mental disorder, the further the person has regressed. Ps_____ seeks to uncover the repressed m_____ so that patients can gain i_____t into their mental disorder. To achieve this they must experience e_____ i_____t with the repressed memories.

Ψ Hypnosis and the treatment of Anna O.

Ψ Free association and resistance.

Ψ Dream analysis—the 'royal road to the unconscious'.

Ψ The role of transference.

Evaluation

Ψ Research evidence that childhood is a source of abnormality (Kendler et al., 1996, and Caspi et al., 1996).

Ψ Insight is important in recovery from mental illness.

Ψ Transference is not a key factor in recovery (Høglend, 2004).

Ψ Psychodynamic therapy is often found to be less effective than later therapies.

Ψ It is the origin of all modern forms of 'talking cures' and so has made an enormous contribution to society.

Ψ The therapist may 'implant' memories, leading to 'false memory syndrome'.

Ψ Difficult to operationalise and so test experimentally the value of insight and transference, which leads to criticisms of scientific validity.

Ψ Too much emphasis on the past and sexual factors and not enough on the current and social factors.

Ψ Ethical issues—where does blame lie?

Systematic desensitisation

Description
This treatment is based on the principles of l_____ and in particular the theory that behaviour is learned through a_____ (c_____ conditioning). Abnormality is a result of learning maladaptive and dysfunctional b_____ and so the treatments it uses counter-c_____ to replace the maladaptive (dysfunctional) behaviour with more a_____ (f_____) behaviour.

Ψ Systematic desensitisation.
- First stage—relaxation training.

- Second stage—fear hierarchy.

- Third stage—imagine feared objects.

- Fourth stage—experience feared objects.

Ψ Requires therapist expertise.

Ψ How does it work? Reciprocal inhibition or extinction?

Evaluation
Ψ Moderate effectiveness.

Ψ Which process is more important: reciprocal inhibition or extinction (McGlynn et al., 1981)?

Ψ A pioneering treatment that paved the way for further behavioural therapies.

Ψ Strong theoretical and scientific basis—variables within the treatment can be manipulated to test experimentally.

Ψ Why does systematic desensitisation have restricted usefulness?

Ψ How does systematic desensitisation compare to exposure and virtual exposure therapy?

Ψ Underlying causes are ignored because the behaviourists refuse to investigate internal processes. They treat only that which is observable and measurable i.e., symptoms not causes.

Notes

NOTES